THE GURU IN SIKHISM

THE GURU IN SIKHISM

W. Owen Cole

Darton, Longman & Todd
London

First published in 1982 by
Darton, Longman & Todd Ltd
89 Lillie Road, London SW6 1UD

© W. Owen Cole 1982

ISBN 0 232 51509 3

British Library Cataloguing in Publication Data

Cole, W. Owen
　The Guru in Sikhism.
　1. Sikh gurus
　I. Title
　294.6'64　　　BL2018

　ISBN 0–232–51509–3

Phototypeset by Input Typesetting, London SW19 8DR
Printed in Great Britain by The Anchor Press Ltd
and bound by Wm Brendon and Son Ltd
both of Tiptree, Essex

To Piara Singh Sambhi, my friend and teacher,
with affection and gratitude

Contents

Abbreviation

AG   Adi Granth

Preface

The term Guru conjures up many pictures in the minds of western readers or even among travellers who have had the privilege of visiting India. Sometimes the mind's eye catches sight of the exotic or of a group of hippies gathered in meditation around a benign, smiling teacher. Recently, the image has been tarnished by stories of commercial or sexual exploitation. The guru is seen as one who makes a living from the gullibility of those who seek a spiritual satisfaction which apparently they cannot find in the material cultures of the west. When my own study of Sikhism began it was reassuring to discover that the founder of that religion, Guru Nanak, was himself a man acutely aware of the temptations which lie before those who, as gurus, exert power and influence upon others. One became surprised at the way in which a whole line of ten Gurus had successfully remained teachers and the preservers of the original teachings of Guru Nanak. Yet this they did despite playing an increasingly social and political part in the life of the India of their day. Even more astonishingly the tenth of these men, Guru Gobind Singh, brought to an end the line of human Gurus by conferring guruship upon the collection of hymns which his followers used in their personal and corporate devotions. So a movement whose focal point was a series of ten men became centred upon a book, henceforward known by the name Guru Granth Sahib, as well as by the original title of Granth or Adi Granth. Yet this is not itself the whole of the story. Guru Nanak had always insisted that God, the ultimately unknowable source of being, had graciously revealed himself to mankind through his word. He was the eternal Guru, Guru Nanak was only his minstrel, the person through whom the message was communicated to mankind.

The story of the Guru in Sikhism is one of tension. On the one hand there are the teachings of the Gurus themselves, on the other, there is the Sikh community attempting to remain loyal to the message but, because the community is composed of human beings, ever in danger of replacing the message with some other allegiance, be it to a human being, the scripture as a physical object, or the Khalsa with the emphasis placed on its outward appearance of the uncut hair and the turban rather than its inner spiritual loyalty to the revelation communicated to and through the Gurus. It is possible to question Sikh children about a picture of Guru Nanak or one of his successors, hanging at home, or in the place where they worship, the gurdwara, and be told, 'He is our God'. It is usual to see a Sikh make a low bow or full prostration before the copy of the scriptures, the Guru Granth Sahib, and treat it with a reverence bordering on worship. It is equally true to say that some eminent spiritual teachers of the Sikh community in the nineteenth or twentieth centuries have been acclaimed as gurus by some members of the religion. However, what is more remarkable is the way that Sikhism has maintained its integrity despite aberrations resulting from popular piety and the fact that for much of its time it has existed as a subculture of Hinduism.

When I decided to channel my initial general exploration into the Sikh religion more narrowly, precisely, and deeply, it took only a little time to decide that my research subject should be the concept or guruship in Sikhism, for it was clear that behind the potent symbols of the pictures of the Gurus and the enthroned Guru Granth Sahib lay a concept which was both rich and complex, and whose significance extends beyond the confines of the study of Sikhism or even of the religious tradition of India. The belief that the Guru is God manifest as Word is one which strikes a chord in Judaism, Christianity and Islam as well as Hinduism. However, the implications that this may have for those interested in religious dialogue is something that I do not intend to touch upon here. Deeply concerned with interfaith and community relations matters though I am, I have resisted the temptation to stray from my primary aim of expounding and analysing the Sikh concept of guruship.

I owe a considerable debt to the many Sikhs I have met who have patiently explained their beliefs and practices to me and have overwhelmed me with their kindness and hospitality. By naming some I hope I will not give offence to others, but it would be disrespectful of me not to mention Professor Harbans Singh, Professor Parkash Singh, Dr S. S. Kohli, Dr Trilochan Singh and above all Dr Gobind Singh Mansukhani. The dedication of this study to Piara Singh Sambhi is the least I can do to acknowledge the kindness of his family to mine and the unstinting advice and help which he has always been prepared to give me.

The initial form of this study was a thesis written for the M.Phil. degree of Leeds University. Dr Ursula King patiently and wisely guided my research. For her help I am deeply grateful. I must also thank Dr King and Professor Parrinder for encouraging me to turn the thesis into a book and John Todd for being willing to publish it. My wife, Gwynneth, deserves special mention for typing the manuscript and probably a public apology for being asked to cope with such dreadful handwriting!

During the period of my research I was also fortunate in being able to discuss aspects of this study with Terry Thomas of the Open University and with Professor Hew McLeod of Otago, whose replies to my many letters of inquiry were always swift and detailed beyond my hopes or deserving.

Any blemishes and shortcomings are as much my fault as the merits are attributable to others. However, I hope my Sikh friends will receive the book with generosity and regard it as an act of homage, however inadequate. Perhaps it will stimulate other readers to deepen their interest in Sikhism.

W. Owen Cole
Chichester
1981

1

The Guru in the Indian Tradition

Sikhism is now a little over 500 years old. Guru Nanak, acknowledged by Sikhs to be the founder of their faith, was born in 1469 and the movement which he originated in the Punjab, though still centred upon that part of India, has now spread to many parts of the world, taken by emigrant Sikhs. It is not a missionary faith, even though Guru Nanak travelled widely communicating his message to those who would listen, establishing congregations of disciples (for which the Punjabi word is 'sikh') wherever he went. Consequently, most Sikhs living outside the Punjab are first, second, third or occasionally fourth-generation migrants who retain Punjabi as a spoken language at home as well as in the gurdwara, read local community newspapers, novels or devotional literature, including the scriptures in Gurmukhi, the written form of Punjabi, and often still possess property in the Punjab to which they frequently make visits. There have been a number of recent conversions to Sikhism, especially in the U.S.A, as a result of personal conviction, not merely as a consequence of mixed marriages; but in order to take a full place in the community the believer must quickly learn its language as well as accepting Punjabi customs of diet and behaviour. The roots of Sikhism are firmly planted in India. It is to that Indian religious tradition that we must turn in our attempt to understand the major distinct concept of Sikhism, that of guruship.

India has seen the emergence of many guru cults in its long history. Many have disappeared soon after the death of the preceptor, the disciples merging again into the tradition from which they were drawn. The guru becomes lost to memory save for a samadhi, a tomb or memorial shrine, and perhaps some devotional verses which he may have composed, passed

1

through the disciples' families sometimes for many generations. Sikhism may be regarded as a gurucult which has persisted and in doing so made a distinctive contribution to the concept of guru in the Indian religious tradition.

The precise meaning of the word guru is uncertain. The Sanskrit dictionary of Monier Williams offers the following definitions: *(adj.)* heavy, weighty, heavy in stomach, (food) difficult to digest, great, large, high in degree, venerable, important, serious, momentous, valuable, haughty, proud; *(noun)* a spiritual parent or preceptor, author of a mantra, preceptor of the gods. Some explanations of the term say that 'gur' means to lift, hurt, kill or eat; therefore the guru is a person who lifts up a disciple by killing, destroying or devouring his ignorance. Another suggestion is that 'gr' means to sing or to swallow; accordingly a guru is so called because he preaches dharma to his disciples or swallows their ignorance. The Aiteraya Upanishad and the Kularnava Tantra assert that 'gu' signifies darkness, 'ru' that which restrains it, so a guru is a restrainer of ignorance. Rather similar to this is the explanation given by a number of Sikhs that 'gu' means 'darkness', 'ru' means 'light'; thus a guru is one who delivers those who accept his teaching and discipline from darkness to enlightenment, from samsara, the road of rebirths, to moksha, spiritual realization and release.

It may be noted that disagreements about the etymology of the term tend to be resolved when it comes to discussing the functions of gurus. Down the ages they have been spiritual preceptors. Gurus are men, and sometimes women, who have become spiritually enlightened and who believe that they have some responsibility to guide others, so helping them to attain moksha. The help which they give may be in the form of knowledge, techniques, or a combination of both, and sometimes by the direct giving of power, shaktipat. However, the hope of a disciple is that expressed in the Brihadaranyaka Upanishad:

> From the unreal lead me to the real,
> From darkness lead me to light,
> From death lead me to immortality. (1.3.28)

The first men to be called gurus, according to Hindu trad-

2

ition, were brahmins who taught Vedic knowledge to boys and young men of the kshatriya and vaisya classes as well as their own. The Laws of Manu, a code of conduct compiled sometime about the third century B.C.E. (before the Common Era), state that a brahmin has the right to study and teach the Vedas, which kshatriyas and vaisyas have a right and duty to study. Implicit in this statement is the view that through knowledge of and obedience to the precepts of the Vedas, moksha is achieved. In contemporary twentieth-century Hindu society the requirements of this code are still met to some extent though usually symbolically, normally only by brahmin families. However, the custom persists of a priest initiating a brahmin into his class through the sacred thread ceremony (upanayam) and receiving the homage due to a guru from the young man. Now the brahmin comes to the home of the initiate, whereas in ancient times the boy went to the dwelling of his teacher whom he would serve for a number of years in return for being educated in the Vedas. The teacher may now impart a mantra – certainly at the initiation ceremony the pupil will formally utter the Gayatri Mantra – but little other education is likely to take place. Among kshatriyas and vaisyas initiation by a brahmin is far less frequently observed than in the past. The brahmin gurus argued that the authority of their message lay in the sacred authority of the words of the Vedas, divinely revealed; the shabad, or word; the expansion of the sacred and primal syllable Om, which is Brahman. They might also trace it to Brahma, as Adi-Guru, the First Teacher. In the Mandaka Upanishad this idea is conveyed by means of genealogy which traces the teaching of Angiras to the first of the gods, Brahma (1.1–2). In the Bhagavad Gita, Krishna the charioteer is eventually seen to be the supreme Brahman, beyond all categories and qualities (nirguna). He is also Arjuna's guru, advising him, commanding him on matters of dharma, but also disclosing Brahman to him and teaching him the highest way to release. Here the guru is Brahman in manifest form (saguna).

Side by side with the tradition of the guru being a brahmin initiating students into Vedic knowledge has developed another which may be derived from it, though it could be of a

3

different origin. Personal spiritual experience is a much emphasized quality in the Indian religions. People who are manifestly enlightened, who also possess the ability to enable others to achieve the goal which they have attained, are greatly respected; their ministry and guidance is widely sought. Such teachers might be brahmins basing their message on the Vedas, or kshatriyas or vaisyas who justify their teaching by tracing it to the Vedas and their right to teach by arguing that many of their predecessors, the gurus of the Upanishads, were not brahmins for in ancient times brahmins were simply men who put aside evil and unwholesome ways for a life devoted to seeking the truth through meditation. So a Buddhist text, the Digha Nikaya (3.80ff.), claiming to quote the Buddha, tries to explain the word brahmin as arising from 'bahenti', meaning 'put away'; 'this was the origin of the brahmins . . . They originated quite naturally and not otherwise.' There is no need to enter into that particular argument in order to make the point that a strong tradition exists of teachers who were not even members of the twice born classes, but who claimed a right to teach based on personal experience. Some of them, like the Buddha, went further than denying the claims of the brahmins; they also rejected the authority of the Vedas. To this group Guru Nanak belongs. He was a bedi-khatri, member of a jati for which kshatriya status is claimed, who, as we shall see, based his right to teach on his personal experience of a command (hukam) received directly from God himself.

Before proceeding to an examination of Guru Nanak's claims and a discussion of what guruship meant to him, it might be helpful to consider the nature and practice of guru cults which exist today, so that the Sikh idea and form may be examined in its Indian context. The Hindu guru owes his authority to the faith of his devotees. In some way he has acquired a reputation as a person who can confer spiritual enlightenment, peace, and possibly occult powers or the ability to cure sickness of the body and the mind. His home, which may be extremely modest or a well-appointed modern house, is the gathering place for people who may come only from nearby villages or who have travelled great distances. Sometimes these seekers will wait many hours for a glimpse

4

of him. They may even stay for days and weeks if they have arrived when he is away on a journey. When at last the guru does appear, each person gathered before him will believe that he or she is looking upon God. Should the guru's benign glance (darshan) fall upon them, they will be conscious of receiving divine blessing or grace.

Often the guru is a holy person whose benefits can be received at a distance, but it is also possible to enter into a closer relationship, that of guru and disciple (guru and sishya or chela in Sanskrit, for which the Punjabi term is sikh). Such devotees live permanently with the guru or come to him at weekends or when they can obtain leave of absence from their employment. In the distant past these temporary visits would have taken place preferably at the time of monsoon or when-ever the demands of making a livelihood were less urgent. Now it may be at any time or when the guru requires it. The guru–chela relationship begins with the prospective disciple seeking a teacher. The motives prompting this search will be both negative and positive in most cases. Dissatisfaction of many kinds may provide the negative spur: a disturbance of the close family relationship which is often sufficient to meet a person's need for security in Indian society, or a rejection of religious and social norms. Positively, the potential disciple will have heard of the guru's reputation and is confident that such a preceptor can meet his needs. The message itself may not be important, so long as it is applicable to the seeker's condition. The relationship of guru and chela is usually per-sonal rather than intellectual, though this does not mean that the teaching is insignificant. However, the devotee's response to the guru consists of personal homage and the use of certain meditative techniques taught by the master. The ability to articulate the guru's message is often slight, expressed in clichés, as piety frequently is. Such faith, nevertheless, should not be dismissed as weak or superstitious.

Diksha, initiation, is conferred by the guru when he con-siders that the disciple is ready. Traditionally the disciple showed his intention by bringing fuel and other gifts to the guru. Acceptance of these offerings indicated that the guru was willing to receive him. Sometimes, however, the seeker may be tested over a long or short period during which his

5

sincerity, obedience and ability to assimilate the teaching are proved. Once the guru is satisfied, initiation may be conferred by giving a mantra (anavi initiation), by touch, word or glance which produces sudden enlightenment (sambhavi) or by the transmission of power (shakti). The chela, for his part, may be given rules of diet, dress and conduct to keep. There may be a rite of initiation. The guru may sprinkle consecrated water on the disciple (abhisheka), or water poured over the guru's feet and collected in a bowl may be administered to the initiate as a drink (charn-amrit).

From this moment, for the rest of his life the chela must be obedient to his guru before anyone else. He belongs to the guru 'tan, man ane dhan', 'body, mind and wealth'. When the disciple enters the guru's presence he will remove his shoes and prostrate (dandaut) himself in front of the guru, who will be sitting on a low stool or cushion. He will place offerings at the guru's feet (charn-puja), and in return be given food (prasad) which is a means of conveying the closeness of the guru–chela relationship in tangible form. In popular writings, much is made of the guru giving his chela betel to chew which has been in his own mouth. Such gifts, when they are made, whould not be noticed for their unhygienic properties or as evidence of the use of narcotics, but as symbols of a relationship. More important is the disciple's growth in understanding the secret doctrine (rahasyn) imparted at initiation and expertise in practising the techniques of realization.

Yoga, a word with many connotations, is a method frequently taught by the guru for attaining divine knowledge and inner peace through harmony with reality. Common features of all yogic routines are the adoption of a meditative posture (asana), controlling the breath and body, and concentrating the mind on a mantra.

Finally, a word must be said about the succession from one guru to another. As a teacher grows old it is not uncommon for him to choose one of his disciples, the person who most fully represents his ideals, prepare him to be his successor and finally nominate him during a ritual which may include inducting him to the guru's gaddi. At the guru's death the disciples believe that his light has passed to his successor, who is considered to be a reincarnation of the master.

Such, in outline, is the place of the guru in the Indian religious tradition, the relationship of preceptor and disciple, and the ritualization of the relationship. In the rest of this book we will examine guruship in the Sikh tradition and then consider it against this background.

Readers wishing to pursue further the theme of guruship in the Indian religious tradition might be interested to study part five, chapter one of *The Speaking Tree* by Richard Lannoy (OUP 1971), which explores the psychological role of gurus, and *Mind, Body and Wealth* by David Pocock (Blackwell 1973), which places the guru in the context of village practice and belief. *The Nature of Guruship*, edited by Clarence O. McMullen (ISPCK, Delhi 1976), considers the Sikh concept alongside that of other Indian religious movements and of Christianity. *Krishna: Myths, Rites and Attitudes*, edited by Milton Singer (University of Chicago 1966), also contains valuable insights which help to place this present study in a wider Indian setting.

2

Guru Nanak

Analytical and descriptive accounts of the lives of the ten Sikh
Gurus are not difficult to find, so it is not proposed to add to
them here. Instead, we will confine ourselves to an examination of some of the major issues of guruship which arise
from the life and work of these men.

Guru Nanak was born in 1469 in the village of Talwandi,
not far from Lahore. Today named Nankana Sahib, out of
respect for its most famous inhabitant, it lies in Pakistan. The
life of Guru Nanak falls into three roughly equal parts: the
years of preparation from his birth until about 1499; the years
of mission during which he travelled widely; and the years of
consolidation from approximately 1521 until his death in
1539. His base for these eighteen or nineteen years was the
village of Kartarpur which he founded.

Attempts to discover the name of Guru Nanak's guru are
apparently as old as his ministry. Often he has been associated with the famous teacher Kabir. This is not altogether
surprising, for some of Kabir's hymns are contained in the
Adi Granth. These reveal considerable agreement with the
Sikh Guru on such issues as caste, ritualism, sectarian religion
and the importance of experiencing God as immanent. Also
there is a tradition in two of the hagiographic 'lives' of Guru
Nanak of a meeting between the two men. Circumstantially,
the evidence seems strong. However, it has to be rejected for
a number of reasons. The biographical evidence is contained
in two different janam sakhis and points in two directions.
The Miharban Janam Sakhi describes a meeting between the
two men at Benares. Each refers to the other as 'God' and
Kabir addresses Guru Nanak as 'jagat Guru' (literally, world
teacher or world enlightener).

The conversation, typically Indian in its politeness, ran as follows:

Kabir   Good God, please be seated. I am not so great that a man of your eminence should stand up to receive me.

Nanak   When a god comes, how can one remain seated?

Kabir   No. No. You are a jagat Guru (world Guru) and I am your slave.

Nanak   Blessed am I that I have met you.

Kabir   You have been sent to save the world, O Nanak.

Nanak   I am not worried about the world. All I wish is that I may not forget God.

Kabir   Yet the world will acknowledge you as a supreme prophet.

Nanak   O Kabir, you serve God. Your deeds are truthful. Your mind is one with Pure Being (niranjan).

Kabir   From whom did you receive the divine light? Who is your guru?

Nanak   I met the Perfect Being, the Supreme Person, the Embodiment of Truth, and have received enlightenment from him. It is only the Perfect Guru, illumined by God, who can save the world.

The question of the historicity of this meeting must remain open. The purpose of this account would seem to be beyond question. It is to show that mutual respect existed between the two men; each regarded the other as a true guru; but it should not be doubted that ultimately Guru Nanak is the greater. Doubtless such a story would be used by Sikhs to persuade Kabir panthis to join them. It may well have been created by the community for this purpose.

The second account is in the Hindaliya Janam Sakhi, which is associated with Bidhi Chand, a contemporary of the sixth Guru, Hargobind (1595–1644). Bidhi Chand married a Muslim woman and became an apostate, apparently as a result of Sikh criticisms of his marriage. The rival movement which he established took the name Hindalis after his father, Baba Hindal, a convert and loyal follower of the third Guru, Amar Das, and a highly respected leader of the community. The Hindali Janam Sakhi contains episodes in which Guru Nanak

9

is denigrated at the expense of Hindal and Kabir. Though Westcott and, through him, other writers have accepted the Hindali account which explicitly states that Guru Nanak was a disciple of Kabir, the overall purpose of this janam sakhi must incline us to doubt this piece of evidence.

The chronology of Guru Nanak is not disputed. That he was born in 1469 and died in 1539 is agreed. Kabir's dates are still the subject of argument.[1] Professor McLeod regards the traditional date of his death, 1518, as 'at least a definite likelihood', but considers the traditional date of his birth, 1398, to be 'highly improbable'. Parasuram Chaturvedi favours 1448 as the date of Kabir's death. In her recent study of Kabir, Professor Vaudeville prefers to accept the view that he lived in the first half of the fifteenth century, on the basis of Professor Chaturvedi's argument. To arrive at a certain conclusion is clearly impossible but two points must be borne in mind. First, early dates given of Kabir's birth are probably influenced by the desire to make him the disciple of Ramanand. Secondly, early dates for Kabir's death may be part of a search for plausibility. The link of Kabir with Ramanand must be considered unlikely, despite the attractiveness of the story of the brahmin guru who, tripping over the prostrate low-caste Kabir in the dark cried out 'Ram' and thereby gave Kabir a mantra, thus was compelled to accept him as a disciple. This must be regarded as an attempt by later followers of Kabir to provide their panth with a brahmin guru to counter the criticisms of such smartas as the poet Tulsi Das,[2] who is reputed to have died in 1623 at the age of eighty. As will be seen later, Kabir belonged to a group of mystics who acknowledged no human guru.

The dates of the two men leave open the possibility of Guru Nanak's being the disciple of Kabir. However, the real issue is the similarity of their teaching. It is this more than anything else which has encouraged scholars to postulate a guru–chela relationship between the two teachers. Perhaps they disagree most on the nature of maya, and Kabir discloses a preference

1 A fuller discussion of the dating of Kabir's life is to be found in McLeod (1968), pp. 155–6 and Vaudeville (1974), pp. 36–9.
2 His view is discussed by Raymond Allchin in his critical introduction to *Kavitavali* (Allen & Unwin 1964), pp. 47–9.

for 'Ram' as a name applicable to God whereas Guru Nanak tends to avoid sectarian names. There may be more place given to hukam, God's will or ordinance, in Guru Nanak's compositions, but on the great issues they are essentially in agreement. The Brahmanical and smarta traditions, the varnashram dharma, sacrifices, pollution, esoteric yogic teaching and worship involving statues are all rejected. On the other hand, positively God is spoken of as creator, the only reality, the one without a second. He is called Sat Guru and worship is by meditation on the divine name, nama japa, even though each of them uses poetry as a means of conveying his message and is consequently regarded as belonging to the bhakti tradition.

Were these two men's teachings unparalleled in Hinduism, the case for Guru Nanak's dependence upon Kabir might be regarded as overwhelmingly convincing. However, an alternative solution seems not only possible but likely. Fairly recently, the attention of scholars has been drawn increasingly to a group of north Indian mystical poets commonly described as sants. This term is normally a synonym for sadhu but in this context it refers to one who believes in a supreme, nonincarnated God. Sometimes those who comprise this group are described as nirguna sampradaya or school, but such an appellation has its difficulties. Two of those who may be included were happy to use sectarian names for God. One of them was Lalla, also known as Lal Ded or Lallesvari woman of the bhangi (scavenger) caste. She was a Saivite yogi, able in her poems to equate Siva with Vishnu-Krishna (Kesava) or Jina, the name given to the karma conquering Mahavira, the founder of Jainism. The other was Kabir, whose use of the name Ram has already been noted.

Lalla, who may have lived in the late fourteenth century, described her spiritual search and the eventual realization of the truth thus:

I wearied myself seeking for him and searching,
I laboured and strove even beyond my strength,
I began to look for him and lo, the bolts were on his door.
And even in me, as I was, did longing for him become fixed:
I there, where I was, I gazed upon him.

11

Elsewhere she relates her spiritual experience as follows:

> With passionate longing did I, Lalla, go forth,
> Seeking and searching did I pass the day and night.
> Then lo, saw I in mine own house a learned man,
> And that was my lucky star and my lucky moment when
> I laid hold of him.

> Slowly, slowly, did I stop my breath in the bellows-pipe
> (of my throat).
> Thereby did the lamp (of knowledge) blaze up within me,
> and then was my true nature revealed unto me.
> I winnowed forth abroad (spread within myself) my inner
> light,
> So that, in the darkness itself, I could seize the truth and
> hold it tight.

The allusion to yoga, suppression of the breath, the awareness of God as immanence after failing to find him outside, in ritualism, is typical of the sants, as is the ultimate realization of reality contained in this next verse:

> He who hath deemed another and himself the same,
> He who hath deemed the day (of joy) and the night (of
> sorrow) to be alike,
> He whose mind hath become free from duality,
> He, and he alone, hath seen the Lord of the Chiefest of the
> Gods.

Even earlier, Namdev (1270–1350), a low-caste calico printer, is reputed to have told a Muslim ruler that 'God is in everything' and expressed his ideas in poetry:

> If I should bring flowers and make them garlands, to honour this idol, the bee has sucked the flowers.
> God is in the bee.
> Where should I weave a garland for his image?
> God is with us here, God is beyond us there.
> In no place is God not.
> Nama bows to the omnipresent who fills the whole earth.

Ramanand (died 1410?), despite his legendary fame as a guru, has left no works of undisputed authenticity. His one com-

12

position included in the Adi Granth would suggest that he is to be included among the sants.

> Whither shall I go? I am happy at home.
> My heart will not go (with me): my mind has become a cripple.
> One day I did have an inclination to go,
> I ground sandalwood, took aloes paste and many perfumes
> And I was proceeding to worship God in a temple,
> When my Guru showed me that God is in my heart.
> Wherever I go, I find only water and stones,
> But thou art equally contained in full in everything . . .
> The Vedas and the Puranas, all have I seen and searched.
> Go ye thither, if God be not here!
> O Satguru, I am a sacrifice unto thee
> Who hast cut away all my perplexities and errors.
> Ramanand's Lord is the all-pervading God
> The Guru's word cuts away millions of karmas. (Adi Granth 1195)

One might summarize the teachings of the sant tradition as being based upon the belief in one supreme, non-incarnated God who is the only eternal reality, 'the one without a second', to quote a phrase popular among them. From this idea are derived the others: negatively, the rejection of varna and jati, for social distinctions must disappear when reality is acknowledged to be one; the rejection of ideas of purity and pollution, for these also break the concept of unity; the dismissal of the efficacy of ritualistic religion, often in bitterly sarcastic terms. The ramification of these views was far reaching. Not only were the brahmin priests no different from anyone else, it was also inconceivable that truth could be locked away in certain books out of the reach of some classes of men and all women and written in Sanskrit. Positively, the doctrine of one supreme reality immanent in everyone meant that spiritual experience, enlightenment and the attainment of liberation lay within the reach of everyone and that this teaching could be conveyed in the vernacular.

Two other characteristics of sant teaching to which we shall return more than once are the refusal of the sants to name and acknowledge any human guru and their inclination to describe God as Satguru. Clearly the failure of any sant to name his or her guru makes it impossible to trace a lineage from Namdev, who may have been the first known member of the sant tradition through to Guru Nanak. However, it would be wrong to think that the teaching (sampradaya) of the group was passed on through the normal guru–chela relationship. What connects the sants is an association of ideas which were passed on from one generation to another through the verses which Namdev, Lalla and others composed. They would be transmitted orally as folk tales, legends or nursery rhymes and customs were passed on, though many of the sants attached importance to the community of holy people, frequently described as the sangat. It may be supposed that families or groups of villagers who gathered to gossip, tell stories and sing devotional songs (kirtan) kept much of this material alive whilst at the same time they gained spiritual sustenance from the teachings.

It would be illogical, to some degree, to expect these sants to have human gurus, for one of the greatest stresses in their sampradaya was that upon the immanence of the divine and the self-disclosure of God. Some of the verses already quoted bring out this feature. It was emphasized most srongly by the use of the word Sat Guru to describe God.

It would be wrong to regard Guru Nanak as merely another example of the sant tradition. Not only would a careful study of the movement, which is beyond the scope of this book, reveal particular interests and nuances of emphasis in the contribution of each teacher, it would also fail to recognize the relationship of their insights to their own personal experience, and the distinctive contribution of Guru Nanak. In him the nirguna sampradaya receives its clearest and most highly articulated expression. More than this, it can be argued that a primary aim of Guru Nanak and his successors was that of uniting in one movement, capable of attracting those Hindus who fell outside the ministrations of the brahmins, or had rejected them, the disparate sant groups.[3]

3 The sant movement is examined in McLeod (1968), pp. 151–8 and Vaudeville (1974), pp. 97–110. See also McLeod's excellent brief essay in *A Cultural History of India*. OUP 1975.

Guru Nanak's ministry probably began in 1499. According to all the janam sakhi accounts he had been brought up in a Hindu home, though the area in which he lived was under Muslim control and as a young man he was employed as accountant to the local Muslim administrator. Though he married and had two sons he seems to have become increasingly preoccupied with religious rather than domestic matters. The expressions of Hinduism and Islam which he found around him do not seem to have satisfied him; on the contrary, the janam sakhis portray him as being scathingly sceptical of their efficacy. There would seem to be no reason for doubting this portrait; it provides a more than sufficient explanation for the spiritual crisis which Nanak experienced, and its resolution.

One day, so the janam sakhis record, Guru Nanak went to bathe in the river Bein near Sultanpur. There was nothing unusual in this. It was the daily custom of many Hindus and still is. However, Nanak disappeared. His servant Mardana, who had been looking after his clothes, became alarmed and informed Daulat Khan, his employer. The river was dragged but Nanak's body was not found. Three days later, however, he reappeared at the point where he had entered the river. To the crowd which gathered, including Daulat Khan, Nanak said nothing. Wearing only a loincloth he left the village, and with Mardana he went to live with some fakirs. The next day he broke his silence with what is probably his best known statement: 'There is neither Hindu nor Mussulman, so whose path shall I follow? I shall follow God's path. God is neither Hindu nor Mussulman and the path which I follow is God's.'

It is said that sometime later Guru Nanak explained what had happened to him as being taken to God's court and escorted into the divine presence. There he had been given a cup of amrit (nectar) and told to drink it. God had said, 'This is the cup of adoration of God's name. Drink it. I am with you. I bless you and I raise you up. Whoever remembers you

3 *cont.* The argument contained in this paragraph is more fully developed in *Sikhism and its Indian Context 1469–1708: The Attitude of Guru Nanak and Early Sikhism to Indian Religious Beliefs and Practices'*. Darton, Longman & Todd 1982.

will enjoy my favour. Go, rejoice in my name and teach others to do so. I have bestowed the gift of my name upon you. Let this be your calling.'

Probably this description is an amplification of the words of one of Guru Nanak's own hymns:

I was a minstrel out of work,
The Lord gave me employment.
The mighty One instructed me,
'Sing my praise, night and day.'

The Lord summoned the minstrel.
To his high court.
On me he bestowed the role of honouring him and singing his praise.

On me he bestowed the nectar in a cup,
the nectar of his true and holy name.
Those who at the bidding of the Guru
Feast and take their fill of the Lord's holiness,
Attain peace and joy.
Your minstrel spreads your glory
By singing your word.
Nanak, through adoring the truth
We attain to the all-highest. (AG 150)

This hymn and the janam sakhi narrative bear witness to a deeply transforming experience, which resulted in the consciousness of being chosen to undertake the mission of revealing the message of God's name to the world. The actual event defies analysis. Probably intentionally the mundane possibility that Guru Nanak slipped away from Mardana to resolve his spiritual crisis alone through meditation is discounted. The emphasis in the story is upon a divine initiative which gave him, an unemployed bard, a task to do and a message to preach. It should be noted here that we are also invited to see God as provider of the message and the experience. No sant acknowledged a human guru, though none seems to have gone quite as far as Nanak in describing so vividly an experience of divine inspiration.

Guru Nanak's consciousness of being called by God manifests itself in a humanity which characterizes the Sikh concept of guruship. Sometimes, it is said, Hindu gurus are regarded as more important than God because without them enlightenment cannot be attained. This almost brahmin-like claim to be essential mediators of enlightenment is absent from the teaching of Guru Nanak and his successors. On the contrary, he said:

> I am the handmaiden of my Lord. I have grasped the feet of my Lord, the life of the world has killed and finished my self-conceit [haumai].
> The omipresent embodiment of supreme light and darling supreme Lord is my very life. (AG 1197)

Again using the metaphor employed in the hymn describing his calling, he said:

> I am the Lord's bard of low birth,
> I am your slave, the dust of your servant's feet. (AG 721)

Using imagery drawn from yoga, possibly because conceit was frequently a characteristic of the mendicant yogis he had in mind, he expressed his state thus:

> O Lord, your fear is my hemp, my mind is the leather pouch. I have become an intoxicated hermit.
> My hands are the cup, and I am hungry to see you,
> O God. Day by day I beg at your door . . . Bless me with alms, Lord, a beggar at your door. (AG 721)

Sometimes he also compared himself to the chartrick bird, the pied cuckoo crying for rain, dashing hither and thither in search of water (for example, AG 1273). For Guru Nanak inspiration was not self-induced. He said,

> As I am given, so I speak. (AG 722)

Otherwise he remained silent.

One of the most interesting incidents recorded in the janam sakhis describes the Mughal siege of Saidpur in 1524. It asserts that Guru Nanak and Mardana were among a group of captives being led from the town. Mardana had been given an officer's horse to look after. As they walked, Guru Nanak

17

became aware of the imminence of an inspired utterance. 'Mardana, touch the chords of your rebeck,' he said, 'the word (bani) is descending.' 'But master,' his companion replied, 'my hands are occupied in holding the reins of this horse. If I let it go, it may run away.' 'Let the horse go,' insisted Guru Nanak, 'the word is descending.' Contemplation and premeditation had their place in Guru Nanak's compositions and in his strategy, but place must also be found for spontaneity of action and thought.

Gurus and self-styled religious teachers, as a group, did not win the admiration of Guru Nanak. He was concerned that their motives were often selfish and spurious.

> One sings religious songs, though he possesses no divine knowledge. A hungry mullah turns his home into a mosque. An idler has his ears pierced – and so becomes a yogi! Another embraces the life of a mendicant to shake off his caste. (AG 1245)

Such spiritual preceptors were to be shunned. They could offer no help. Perhaps the criterion of a true guru lies in the sentence which follows those words of denunciation:

> He who eats what he earns through honest toil and gives some of what he has in charity; he alone, Nanak says, knows the true way of life. (AG 1245)

Between 1499 and about 1521, throughout India and beyond, Guru Nanak spent much of his time preaching the message which had been entrusted to him. The janam sakhis describe journeys to Sri Lanka, Tibet, Baghdad and even Mecca. The conviction which compelled and inspired him came from his enlightenment and commissioning experience. It is less easy to explain how he came by his teaching. Clearly the janam sakhi narrative and the hymn quoted above assert that he received it, the nectar of God's name, from God himself. But what of its form and content? It must be surmised that Guru Nanak became familiar with the nirguna sampradaya before his enlightenment, that he began to preach only when he was certain of his commitment to it and convinced that he had been given the task of preaching. India has many sadhus,

18

people seeking to deepen their own spiritual awareness. It has had many gurus, some self-styled, others like Guru Nanak who were reticent to claim the title. Significantly there is no evidence that Guru Nanak ever applied the term guru to himself.

Guru Nanak may have first come across sant teachings through his contacts with holy men of different persuasions. However rigorously one may analyse the janam sakhis, however sceptical one may be of particular incidents, nevertheless they do provide pointers towards his interest and methods of teaching. The stories of his young adulthood before his Sultanpur experience suggest that he spent much of his time – too much for his father's liking – seeking the company of holy men. It was lack of attention to his family responsibilities and to business, and the young man's unhealthy introspection which prompted his father to send him to his sister, Nanaki. They had always been close; perhaps she could take him out of himself, and her husband Jai Ram could procure him employment. If the young man did not meet Kabir, and we have argued that no reliable historical evidence for such an encounter exists, he must have learned of him and probably of other sants from some of the men he met and questioned. However, it seems likely that, at some point, Guru Nanak took his interest in the sants further and probably collected many of their verses.

In order to consider this possibility it is necessary to leap forward in time to 1604. In that year the first definitive collection of Sikh writings, known as the Adi Granth, was compiled by Guru Arjan. It contained the compositions of his four predecessors and his own hymns, arranged in thirty ragas. There were in addition 541 sabads of Kabir, who came from the jullaha jati which had converted to Islam from Hinduism. Next came sixty hymns by the Hindu tailor or calico printer Namdev and forty-one sabads by Ravidas (Raidas) the chamar. All three of these men are regarded as members of the sant tradition. One hundred and thirty-four hymns of the Sufi Sheikh Farid (1173–1265) were also included in the book. Besides there were some two dozen other

19

sabads composed by twelve other Hindus, including Raman-and (one) and Jai Dev (two).

Guru Arjan did not collect this material himself. Most of it was already in the two books known as the Mohan Pothi compiled at the instruction of the third Guru, Amar Das, sometime earlier than 1574. It is an interesting possibility that Guru Amar Das was responsible for collecting the bhagat bani, to use the convenient Sikh term for the non-Sikh material. However, the compositions of Farid and a number of Guru Nanak's hymns are missing from the Pothi. This may mean that a third volume once existed which is now lost. Otherwise it invites the conclusion that the Farid bani was collected by someone other than Gur Amar Das.[4]

That person could have been Guru Nanak. There is one clear piece of evidence that Guru Nanak knew at least one of Sheikh Farid's hymns. Page 794 of the Adi Granth contains this verse by Farid:

> You would not make a raft at the time when you should have made it. When the sea is full and overflowing, it is hard to cross. Do not touch the saffron flower with your hands, its colour will fade, my dear. First the bride herself is weak and in addition her husband's command is hard to bear. As the milk does not return to her breast, so the soul does not enter the same body again.
>
> Says Farid, my friends, when the spouse calls, the soul departs crestfallen and this body becomes a heap of ashes.

Guru Arjan, when he compiled the Adi Granth, did not juxtapose a hymn which must have been Guru Nanak's response to Farid. It is placed on page 729 of the Sikh scripture.

> Make meditation on the Lord and self-control the raft by which you cross the flowing stream. Your path shall be as comfortable as if there were no ocean or overflowing stream.

4 This is the view expressed by Cole and Sambhi (1978), p. 47. Khush-want Singh (1963), Indian edn (1977), p. 53, states that Guru Amar Das added to the hymns of Nanak and Angad 'his own compositions and those of the Hindu Bhaktas whose teachings were in conformity with those of Nanak'.

Your name alone is the unfading madder with which my cloak is dyed. My beloved Lord, this colour is everlasting. The dear friends have departed, how shall they meet the Lord? If they are united in virtue, the Lord will pin them with himself. Once united, the mortal does not separate again if the union is true. The true Lord puts an end to birth and death.

She who removes self-centredness sews herself a garment to please her husband. By the Guru's instruction she obtained the fruit of the nectar of the Guru's word.

Says Nanak, my friends, my spouse is very dear to me. We are the Lord's handmaiden. He is the true husband.

Of course it is conjecture that Guru Nanak was responsible for gathering the bhagat bani but someone did, before the time of Guru Arjan. Guru Nanak was probably the person with the best motive. If it was his intention to bring together in one coherent group or panth the disparate followers of the teachings of Kabir, Namdev, Ravidas and others, as well as those inclining to Islam under the influence of Sufism, there could be no better way than to give their hymns a place alongside his own when Sikhs gathered to sing kirtans. Finally, in Bhai Gurdas's account of Guru Nanak's journey to Mecca (Var 1.32) we are told that qazis and mullahs gathered round the Guru and questioned him about religion. They opened the book (kitab) which he was carrying and approved of it when they discovered that its contents were religious. Whether Guru Nanak actually visited Mecca or not is a controversy which is irrelevant to our discussion here. The statement that he took a collection of hymns is interesting. Perhaps it reflects a tradition that Guru Nanak had compiled such a collection and was meant to assure Muslims that Sikhism was acceptable to Islam. After all, the religious teachers of their holy city had recognized his authentic spirituality and found no fault with his book of teachings. Bhai Gurdas was the amanuensis of Guru Arjan and wrote the Adi Granth at his instruction. The words in his Var may indicate his acceptance of a tradition that Guru Nanak was the first person to begin a written collection of hymns for Sikh use.[5]

5 An account of the visit is found in Macauliffe, vol. 1, pp. 175–6, Trilochan Singh (1969), p. 380. See also McLeod (1968), pp. 122–5 and
Banerjee (1971), pp. 137–9.
Bhai Gurdas says:
  Baba [Nanak] then proceeded to Mecca, decked in blue garments
  (like) Vishnu banavari [i.e. vanamali, garlanded]. He carried a staff
  in his hand, a book under his arm, a waterpot and a prayer carpet
  (for) the call to prayer (Var 1.32).
  In the next verse the Guru expresses a thought reminiscent of the
  words of Sheikh Farid quoted above: 'The saffron's pigment is not
  fast: it runs when washed with water.'

The Historical Development of Guruship from 1539 to 1708

When Guru Nanak was a little more than fifty years old, probably in 1520, he entered upon the third phase of his life. He founded Kartarpur, a village in the district of Sialkot where he resided until his death in 1539, surrounded by his disciples. Here a distinctively Sikh way of life developed. Its characteristics were, first, that its basis was the householder (grihastha) mode of living. Sikhism is a religion of the family, not one which requires celibacy or detachment from society at some stage. The unmarried adult Sikh is still regarded as an anomaly by the community. Secondly, its focus was the Guru himself but more particularly his hymns which were sung daily, morning and evening, in private and public meditation and worship. Bhai Gurdas, writing early in the seventeenth century, provided this description of the first Sikh community:

> Baba (Nanak) then proceeded to Kartarpur and put aside all the garments of renunciation. He clad himself in ordinary clothes, ascended his gaddi and thus appeared (before his people). He shattered the old tradition and (before his death) appointed Angad as Guru, because his sons did not obey him (becoming instead) perfidious rebels and deserters.
> He gave utterance to words (of divine wisdom) bringing light and drawing away darkness. (He imparted) understanding through discourses and conversation; the unstruck music (of devotional ecstasy) resounded endlessly. Sodar and Arati were sung, and in the early morning the Japji was recited. Those who followed him cast off the burden of the Artharva Veda. (Var 1.38)

Distinctive though this was, it was grafted on to a Hindu cultural pattern from which Sikhism has never fully extracted itself.

At Kartarpur, Sikh guruship began to acquire another characteristic. Besides being a spiritual preceptor, Guru Nanak was a community leader responsible for day-to-day affairs. Although no details of issues he faced or the decisions he took have been preserved, this was an aspect of guruship which was to acquire considerable importance during the period from 1539 to 1708, especially in the late seventeenth century. Guru Nanak prepared the way for it by founding Kartarpur and appointing a successor, Guru Angad, though it was not until leadership passed to the third Guru that political aspects of guruship became significant.

Guru Amar Das (1552–74) made a number of decisions intended to give the Panth greater coherence. He commanded the Sikhs to assemble at Goindwal, where he had established his gaddi, three times a year. The occasions he chose were Maghashivatri, Baisakhi and Diwali. The first and last are festivals dedicated to Siva and Vishnu or Durga, while Baisakhi marks the new year in the Punjab and the beginning of the spring harvest. Sikhs would have to choose between celebrating with their families in Hindu villages and coming, as Sikhs, to their Guru. At Goindwal also he had a baoli or well made, with steps leading down to it. The number of steps is eighty-four, corresponding to the lakhs of rebirths which the atman is said to experience in the Hindu tradition. While pilgrims are taught that only the person who recites the Japji once on each step with sincerity of intention will attain liberation by bathing at Goindwal, nevertheless it must be concluded that Guru Amar Das had the baoli dug to provide Sikhs with an alternative place of pilgrimage to Hardwar or Benares. The decision to construct the well should be regarded as evidence of the success of the Sikh movement which now had to meet the problem of mass conversions.

To keep the Panth permanently united, Guru Amar Das also introduced a system of dividing the scattered communities into twenty-two districts known as manjis (literally 'string bed', but meaning 'seat of authority'). The person appointed to a manji was called a massand. These people were responsible for missionary work and the spiritual welfare of Sikhs in their district. Under Guru Arjan they also collected the das-wand and other tithes imposed by the Guru. At Kartarpur the young Sikh community had practised commensality. Wherever Guru Nanak went, he ate with Hindu or Muslim irrespective of caste and expected those who accepted his teachings to implement them practically by ignoring restrictions upon social interaction. Guru Amar Das institutionalized commensality in the form of langar, a free communal kitchen, establishing the principle 'Pehl pangat, piche sangat', 'First eat together, then meet together' (for discussion or worship). The purpose of langar in those days was more to stress social equality than to feed the hungry, though the charitable motive was doubtless present.

The third Guru also intervened in political issues beyond the limits of the Panth. He persuaded the Mughal government to abolish the tax imposed on pilgrims going to Hardwar and also successfully petitioned the Emperor Akbar to remit taxes in the Lahore district of the Punjab. The imperial army had been campaigning in the region for about a year, with the result that food had become scarce and costly. From this time Sikh affairs became increasingly linked with those of the Mughal Empire.

Guru Ram Das led the Sikh community for only seven years (1574–81). During this time he moved from Goindwal to a place some twenty-five miles away, where he began to construct another well. This task was completed by his son, Guru Arjan, who constructed a building known as the Darbar Sahib or Harmandir and developed a town around it. He also built three other towns: Taran Taran; Kartarpur in the Jullundur Doab; and Shri Hargobindpur on the river Beas. These four towns lie in or near the Majha, a region of the central Punjab which has a high proportion of Jats. Members of this democratic, militant, rural and agrarian community, consisting largely of peasants and landlords, seem to have been entering the Sikh Panth from the time of Guru Amar Das, perhaps causing the balance of influence to shift from the mercantile, urban Khatri group to which the Gurus belonged and from which many of the first Sikhs came. The urbanization of the Majha may be seen as part of a policy to

25

keep control of the Panth and maintain its unity. The same motive may have been behind Guru Gobind Singh's institutionalizing of armed force when he formed the Khalsa in 1699. However, this can only be considered when another political aspect of Sikh guruship has been examined.

There is a tradition that from the time of Ram Das the Gurus were addressed by the title Sachapadsha, True Emperor, a term used by the Mughal rulers.[1] At first, relations between Guru and emperor, Sikh and Muslim were good. Attempts to provoke jealousy and suspicion were made, but without success. When Akbar was told that the newly compiled Adi Granth contained material defamatory to Islam, Bhai Gur Das and Bhai Buddha were able to reassure him. His own scrutiny of the book pleased him so much that he made a large offering of money to Guru Arjan. However, within two years Akbar was dead and the Guru had died in Mughal capivity. Upon Akbar's death the succession was disputed between Khusrau and Jehangir. When the latter had asserted his authority he had Guru Arjan arrested, accusing him of supporting the unsuccessful claimant. While being transported from one place of interogation to another, the Guru was drowned. Though Muslims have always protested that this was an accident, or even that the Guru committed suicide, Sikh opinion is unanimous in regarding it as an act of murder. Guru Arjan is the protomartyr of the Sikh faith.

His son, Guru Hargobind, composed no hymns, kept a small standing army, and occasionally hunted with the Mughal Emperor, though he also suffered a period of imprisonment which perhaps lasted for two years. It is said that when he was released he succeeded in obtaining the liberty of fifty-two Hindu rajas.[2] From this event, which is commemorated by Sikhs at Diwali, dates the tradition which regards Sikhism as a movement dedicated to human rights and resistance against injustice. The martyrdom of the ninth Guru, Tegh Bahadur, in 1675 was interpreted in the same way by his son, the tenth Guru:

To protect their right to wear the

1 Macauliffe, vol. 2, p. 271.
2 Khushwant Singh (1977 edn), vol. 1, p. 64.

26

tilak and sacred thread,
He in the Dark Age [Kal Yug], performed
the supreme sacrifice.
To help the saintly he went to the
utmost limit.
He gave his head but remained resolute. ('Vachitar Natak')

The tenth Guru's own struggles are explained as a dharm yudh, the kind of fight conducted by Rama against Ravana, or by the Pandavas against the usurping Kauravas in the Mahabharata.

The distinctive development of a political role by the Sikh Gurus may be explained in part as an attempt to control and discipline their more militant members, though there would seem to be sufficient evidence available to argue that the Gurus themselves were willing political as well as spiritual leaders. Perhaps in the historical context it was virtually inevitable that a growing religious movement which emphasized unity and allegiance to a Guru should be considered a political threat by the Mughals or that the nishan sahib of the Guru should become a rallying standard for those in the Punjab who were hostile to it. However, a factor as strong as that of pressures within the Panth may have been the policies of the different emperors. Perhaps this can be shown by contrasting the attitude of Guru Arjan when his son Hargobind was born and that of Guru Gobind Singh when he established the Khalsa.

Guru Arjan's marriage had been childless. He was forty-two and had been Guru for fourteen years. His elder brother, Prithi Chand, who had never accepted his father's decision that Arjan should be Guru, was hopeful that one day the gaddi would be his. He was already compiling an anthology of hymns, including his own, as a foundation of his claim to lead the Panth. Then in 1695, Guru Arjan's wife gave birth to a son. The hymn which greeted his birth may have been influenced by relief and fatherly pride, but it also reveals a sense of destiny.

The true Sat Guru has sent the child.
The long-lived child has been born by destiny.
When he came and acquired an abode in the world his

27

mother's heart became very glad.
The son, the saint of the world-Lord (Gobind) is
born. The primal writ had become manifest among all.
In the tenth month, by the Lord's command, the baby
had been born. Sorrow has left and great joy has
become manifest.
The Sikhs sing the gurbani in their joy. (AG 396)

In the tolerant empire of Akbar who has been called one of
the supreme architects of a Hindu–Muslim synthesis,[3] it may
be that Guru Arjan believed that Sikhism might be a faith
which would unite India.

Ironically, that aspiration was dashed with the Emperor's
death and the Guru's martyrdom. At the formation of the
Khalsa, nearly a century later in 1699, the idealism expressed
by Guru Gobind Singh was a bid for unity within the Panth.

> I wish you all to embrace one creed and follow one path,
> obliterating all differences of religion. Let the four Hindu
> castes who have different rules laid down for them in the
> shashtras abandon them altogether and, adopting the way
> of co-operation, mix freely with one another. Let no one
> deem himself superior to another. Do not follow the old
> scriptures. Let none pay heed to the Ganges and other
> places which are considered holy in the Hindu religion, or
> adore the Hindu deities, such as Rama, Krishna, Brahma
> or Durga, but let all believe in Guru Nanak and his suc-
> cessors. Let men of the four castes receive baptism, eat out
> of the same vessel, and feel no disgust or contempt for one
> another.[4]

A janam sakhi account states that Guru Nanak interceded
with the Emperor Babur for the release of prisoners taken
during the destruction of Saidpur when the Mughal army
was invading India. The tradition of political involvement by

3 *Cultural Heritage of India* vol. 4 (Calcutta 1956), p. 582.
4 Khushwant Singh (1977 edn), vol. 1, p. 85. It should be noted that
  Ghulam Mohiuddin (also known as Bute Shah) wrote his history of the
  Sikhs (Tawarikh-i-Punjat) at the request of Dr Captain Murray of the
  East India Company. The date on the manuscript is 1848. There is,
  apparently, no evidence that the author had access to eyewitness
  material.

the Gurus is regarded by Sikhs as an integral aspect of guruship. Their leaders were responsible for the everyday welfare of mankind as well as for their spiritual needs. Their concept of truth included justice, as part of right living, as well as sincere worship.

The Spiritual Development of Guruship after Nanak

The emphasis given to the Gurus' concern with political and social issues between 1539 and 1708 should not encourage the conclusion that no spiritual developments in guruship took place during this period. On the contrary, there were many.

Perhaps most important was the growth in self-awareness. Guru Nanak appears modest and in their hymns his successors manifest the same characteristics of humility and self-deprecation. This attitude persists despite increasingly lavish ceremonies at which Gurus seem to have been enthroned rather than installed, and the picture which emerges of Guru Hargobind ruling more as prince than spiritual leader. More typical of the Gurus than Arjan's eulogy on the birth of his son, were such utterances as these:

> On the basis of his own account the mortal can never be released, for he errs every moment. Pardoner, pardon me and float Nanak across the world ocean. (AG 261)

says Guru Arjan himself, who elsewhere confesses,

> The Lord has forgiven me, his meritless and humble minstrel. (AG 1097)

Guru Ram Das also used the popular bardic analogy, to describe himself:

> We are minstrels of God, our Lord and master. Daily we sing the songs of God's praise. Sing God's praise and the excellence of God, the Lord of wealth and listen to the songs of praise. The Lord alone is the giver. The world is but a mummer. Mortals and other beings are mere beggars. (AG 650)

Guru Tegh Bahadur, probably to emphasize the dependence upon God of all men and women, even a guru, frequently spoke humbly of himself:

29

O my mother, I have not shed the ego of my mind. I have spent my life intoxicated by wealth and have not given myself to meditating upon the Lord. When death's mace falls upon my head, only then will I waken from my slumber. What use is it to repent at that time? Then I cannot escape by running away. When this anxiety wells up in a man's mind he comes to love the Guru's feet. When I become absorbed in the Lord's praise, then only does my life become profitable, says Nanak. (AG 1008)

However, there is evidence that the Panth was given to making embarrassingly extravagant claims on behalf of its leaders. Guru Nanak had called the age in which he lived the Kal Yug, the fourth and most corrupt period (Kalpa) in the Hindu cyclical sequence of time. Its characteristics were the forgetting, neglect or open flouting of dharma, resulting in political upheaval, social collapse, and the suppression of true piety. Guru Nanak reserved some of his sharpest phrases to comment on the age:

The Kalyug is a knife, the rajas are butchers, dharma has taken wings and flown. In this dark night of falsehood the moon of truth cannot be seen rising anywhere. In my search I have become bewildered. In the darkness I find no path. (AG 145)

The Kalyug is a truly wonderful age! A blind man is called an assayer, the counterfeiter called genuine; the worth of the genuine is not even recognized. (AG 229)

In this Kalyug men have faces like dogs. Their food is carrion. They bark falsehood. They have forsaken all thoughts of dharma. (AG 1242)

The world's places of worship are polluted. In this way the world is drowning. In the Kalyug the most sublime thing is the Lord's name. (AG 662)

It can be argued that Guru Nanak regarded himself as God's messenger proclaiming Nam in the Kalyug, but nowhere is the claim explicitly made by him. However, by the time of Guru Arjan the court bards were unrestrained in their acclamation. The bard Kal wrote:

O Guru Nanak, you are blessed with the nectar of the Lord's name and enjoy both the temporal and spiritual realms. In the Satyug you were the dwarf avatar, who defeated King Bal.[5] In the Tretayug you were Ramchandra of the Raghva dynasty. In the Dwapuryug, becoming Krishna, you killed Mur the demon and delivered Kansa. You blessed Ugar Sain with empire and the pious with fearlessness. In the Kalyug you are called and recognized to be the Gurus Nanak, Angad and Amar Das.

Imperishable, immovable is the role of the revered Guru [Sri Guru] for such is the Primal Lord's decree. (AG 1390)

A few lines later the bard asserts that Namdev, Kabir, Ravidas and other poets sang Nanak's praise, together with Mahadev (Siva), Brahma, King Bal and the great yogis.

The bard Kal clearly presents Guru Nanak as an avatar, perhaps the final one, though he does not use the name Kalki. Probably the best and simplest statement of the purpose of an avatar is found in the Bhagavad Gita (4.6 – 8), where the Eternal Being, in the form of Krishna, says:

Unborn am I, changeless is my Self;
Of all contingent beings I am the Lord!
Yet by my creative energy I consort with Nature – which is mine – and come to be in time.

For whenever the law of dharma withers away
and lawlessness [adharma] raises its head,
Then do I generate Myself on earth.

For the protection of the good,
For the destruction of evildoers,
For the setting-up of righteousness,
I come into being, age after age. (Hindu Scriptures, p. 267)

For the bard Bal, Guru Nanak was God himself (Purrukh: a form of the Sanskrit Purusha).

Together with this view that the human Gurus were God manifest, goes the belief that their births were non-karmic. Ordinary mortals are bound to take birth as a consequence

5 In Hindu mythology the defeat of Bal took place in the Tretayug, the second, not the first of the four Kalpas.

of karma accumulated in previous lives. If they become enlightened they must nevertheless continue living until their
karma is exhausted, at which point they will go through the
process known as dying. It is one of the tenets of Sikhism that
a person may become jivan mukt, that is, spiritually liberated
while in the flesh, a fully realized being who will accumulate
no further karma. However, in popular Sikhism the belief
developed that Guru Nanak was not a human being who
became enlightened but an enlightened being who became
reincarnated in obedience to God's command (hukam). The
Sultanpur experience of being taken to God's court was not
one of becoming enlightened but one of being commissioned.
Such stories in the janam sakhis as those which describe the
boy Nanak surpassing his Hindu and Muslim tutors, or even
smiling at birth like a sage, are intended to convey the idea
that the child was already enlightened. According to Sikh
tradition it is not only appropriate but proper, therefore, to
attach the epithet 'Guru' to Nanak's name from the beginning
and to date his guruship and the foundation of the Sikh
movement from his birth in 1469.

In or about 1692[6] Guru Gobind Singh composed an autobiographical poem known as 'Vachitar Natak', 'The Wonderful Drama'. The hymn describes God's plan of deliverance.
The power of Vishnu, Siva, yoga and circumcision is rejected.
The shashtras too are ineffective, as only God's grace can
avail. After this preamble the Guru discloses his intention of
relating his own history and that of his (Sodhi) family, but
first he makes a statement which is relevant to an understanding of later important sections. He writes:

> At first when God extended himself,
> the world was created by him.
> The man who does good deeds is called
> a demigod in this world. He who does
> bad deeds is styled a demon. (Macauliffe p. 290)

Then follow references to mythical and legendary figures,

---

6 This is the date given by Macauliffe, vol. 5, p. 1, note 1. If it does
   pre-date the establishment of the Khalsa in 1699, it suggests that
   panthic ideas had been formed in his mind before it became a formal
   reality.

Kalsain, Aj, Rama and Sita among them. Sita had two sons, Lahu and Kushu, from whom Kalvai and Kalket were descended. They quarrelled and Kalvai fled to the region near Benares called Sanandh, hence the name Sodhi, and from this family the Sodhi dynasty of Gurus was born. From the Kushu family came the Bedi family, which eventually became reconciled to the Sodhis and persuaded its chief, who had gained a kingdom, to become a sannayasin! This Bedi blessed the Sodhi chief, saying:

> When I come in the Kalyug under the name
> of Nanak, I will make you worthy of the worship
> of the world, you shall obtain the highest dignity.
> You have heard the three Vedas from us. On
> hearing the fourth, you gave up your land. Having
> assumed three births in the fourth, I will make you
> Guru. So, the Sodhi king went to the forest and
> the Bedi king was happy with his sovereignty. (Macauliffe
> pp. 293–4)

The story of the Bedi decline is swiftly told to the point where Nanak is born into a farming family. The sequence of Gurus is covered briefly until, finally, the poem becomes autobiographical with the following impressive utterance:

> I shall now tell you my own history,
> How God brought me into the world as I was performing austerities on the mountain of Hemkunt where the mountain peaks are conspicuous, at Sapt Shring where King Pandu practised yoga.
> There I performed great austerities, worshipped Maha Kal and so became blended with God.
> My father and mother had also worshipped the unseen one and strove in many ways to unite themselves with him. The Supreme Guru was pleased with their devotion to him. When God gave me the order I assumed birth in this Kalyug. I did not desire to come, as my attention was on God's feet. God remonstrated with me and sent me into the world . . . (Macauliffe, p. 296)

Before the Guru discloses the instructions he had received from God, he repeats the divine discourse in which God deplores the waywardness and pride of both the good who made themselves gods and the bad who declared themselves to be demons. Siddhas and Sadhus were created but did not find God. The rishis wrote their own smrti instead of following the Vedas. Gorakh, Ramanand and Muhammad were no better, each created his own way. The command to Gobind Rai is, therefore,

I have glorified you as my son, I have created you to proclaim the panth. Go spread the faith there and restrain the people from folly.

The Guru stood up, made obeisance and replied:

This panth I will spread in the world when you give assistance.

To the reader, he continues:

For this reason the Lord sent me; then I took birth and came into the world. What he spoke, that I speak, and I bear no enmity to anyone. Those who call me Parmeshur (Supreme Being) shall all fall into the pit of Hell. Know me as God's servant only – have no doubt of that. I am the slave of the Supreme Being, and have come to behold the spectacle of the world: what the Lord told me, that I tell the world, and I will not remain silent for fear of mortals. (Macauliffe p. 299)

Its martial concern is obvious for it begins with an eulogy on the sword. That it is satirical is less clear. There is certainly an element of Punjabi humour in the description of Bedi–Sodhi relations and the eagerness of the Bedi antecedents of Nanak, the grhastha–sannyasin, to obtain a kingdom! However, the real importance of the poem, in the context of guruship, lies in the assertions that both the Bedi Guru, Nanak and the Sodhi Gurus from Ram Das to Gobind Singh, were descended from Rama and that they were born in response to the divine commandment (hukam), not as the natural consequence of the law of karma. Furthermore, the mission of Guru Gobind Singh was not to restore dharma, as Krishna did in the Bhagavad Gita, but to reveal God, 'to proclaim the

34

panth, to spread the faith'. He is to accomplish what the rishis and Siddhas, Gorakh and Ramanand had failed to do.

In the Sikh bards, as exemplified by Kal, we see a natural inclination to take reverence to the point of worship expressing itself. In Guru Gobind Singh there is a willingness to play with the concept of avatar in order to boost the morale and strengthen the martial spirit of his followers. We may say that the Guru believed in destiny and stated that belief poetically, and with poetic licence in 'Vachitar Natak'; however, it would be wrong to say that he considered himself to be an avatar in the Hindu sense of the word.

The Swayyas, verses used in the Sikh initiation ceremony, contain Guru Gobind Singh's explicit and complete rejection of belief in an incarnate God:

> You say that God is unconceived and unborn; how could he have been born in Kausalya's womb? If he whom we call Krishna were God, why was he subject to death? Why should God whom you describe as holy and without enmity have driven Arjuna's chariot? Worship as God him whose secret none has known or shall know.

> Say, if Krishna were the ocean of mercy, why should the hunter's arrow have struck him? If he can save other families why did he destroy his own? Say, why did he who called himself the eternal and the unconceived, enter the womb of Devaki? Why did he who had no father or mother call Vasudev his father? (Swayyas 13 and 14)

In these passages and elsewhere in the verses of Guru Gobind Singh and in the Adi Granth the Sikh Gurus express the belief that the so-called gods are merely legendary heroes. The bardic assertions that the Gurus are the Ram Chandra or Krishna of the Kalyug are allowed a place in the Sikh scriptures but only in the context of the ancient gods being reduced to mortal status, heroic perhaps, but none the less human for that. They failed in their task of permanently restoring righteousness. So, through wise men, Siddhas, Gorakh, even Muhammad, god made further attempts, but they too failed to establish true religion. Therefore the Sikh Gurus of heroic pedigree were sent to spread the faith and restrain the people from folly. A contemporary of the tenth Guru, named Gur Das (not the famous nephew of Guru Amar Das), said, 'Guru Gobind appeared as the tenth avatar . . . he established the Khalsa as his own sect.' This statement can only be accepted in the context of this revised and severely reduced concept of avatar. Perhaps the last word on this issue should be that of Guru Arjan:

> The omnipresent Lord is without birth and death. Preparing sweets, you give them to stonegods to eat. Ignorant mammon worshipper, the Lord is not born and does not die.
> The faults are endless which come from singing lullabies to stonegods. Burnt be the mouth which says that the Lord enters into existence. He is not born, he does not die. He does not come, he does not go. Nanak says, the Lord is all-pervading. (AG 1136)

Though Sikhs would object vociferously to calling Guru Gobind Singh 'the tenth avatar', the relationship which existed between the Gurus was of great interest to the community in the years following Guru Nanak's death. Bhai Gurdas provided this explanation of the succession of Guru Angad to Nanak:

> Before he died he installed Lehna (as his successor) and set the Guru's canopy over his head. Merging (his) light in (Guru Angad's) light, the Sat Guru changed his form. None could comprehend (this mystery): a wonder of wonders he revealed! Changing his body he made (Guru Angad's) body his own. (Var 1.45)

With more extravagance of language the court bards Satta and Balwand, contemporaries of Bhai Gurdas, wrote in the Coronation Ode:

> Nanak placed the royal umbrella over Angad's head, who praising God, drank divine nectar. The Guru placed the soul-illuminating, supremely powerful sword of his instruction in Lehna's mind. During his own lifetime Guru Nanak made obeisance to Angad, his disciple. The king invested his follower with the tika [mark of authority]. (AG 966)

36

This, the bards said, was like making the river Ganges flow in the opposite direction!

One suspects that Satta and Balwand were contrasting the humility of Guru Nanak, who paid homage to his installed disciple, with the attitude of those like Prithi Chand, who in the time of Guru Arjan apostatized, turning to other leaders or setting up rival movements. To meet this situation a doctrine of unity was formulated. Bhai Gurdas spoke of Guru Nanak's light merging in Angad's. Satta and Balwand said:

> The same is the divine light, the same is the life form. The king has merely changed the body. (AG 966)

Throughout the Adi Granth this belief is expressed through the device of using the formula Mahala I[7] to denote the hymns of Guru Nanak; Mahala II for those of Guru Angad; III for Amar Das; IV for Ram Das; V for Arjan and IX for Tegh Bahadur. Sometimes this designation is abbreviated to MI, MII, or even simply I or II. Within individual hymns Gurus often used the typical expression 'Nanak says', whether the author was Nanak himself or one of the other five Gurus whose hymns are found in the Adi Granth. The belief that the Gurus agreed completely in matters of doctrine is fundamental to Sikhism. It is frequently to be found expressed in articles which examine the transition of Sikhism from being, as many suppose, a pacifist movement under Guru Nanak to be one accepting the need for use of outward force during the reign of Guru Gobind Singh. In these articles strenuous attempts are made to show that in principle the two shared a common aversion to the use of outward force but were even more of a mind that evil must be resisted. While the view of justice is a fundamental of Sikhism, it must be recognized that no evidence exists for adducing Guru Nanak's position on the issue of pacifism.

Throughout the seventeenth century the concept of personal guruship was confronted by two sharply contrasting

---

7 The word 'mahala' can mean a quarter or district of a town. The Guru Granth Sahib is compared to a city and the hymns of each Guru are wards of it. (See Macauliffe, vol. 1, p. 71.) 'Mahala' can also mean bride and thus conveys the idea that each of the Gurus was God's bride; that is the faithful transmitter of the divine message.

pressures. The first and most prominent was to become the focus of political opposition to Mughal rule. Sikhism could easily have become synonymous with the resistance struggle and have forsaken the way of Guru Nanak completely. The second was that of reverting to Hinduism through its Gurus joining the long line of men who had accepted the status of avatar. Somehow the Gurus avoided the extremes and the Panth remained distinctive. The ideal of Guru Nanak, enshrined in the janam sakhis, many of which originated in the seventeenth century, may be the greatest single reason why Sikhism resisted these two pressures.

4

The Concept of Guru in the Teachings of Guru Nanak

Before Guru Nanak's understanding of the concept of Guru can be appreciated, it is necessary to consider aspects of his doctrine of God. This is expressed very tersely in the Mool Mantra, the nearest statement that Sikhism has to a creed. Traditionally it is regarded as Guru Nanak's first poetic utterance after his commissioning experience at Sultanpur. Sikhs are formally taught it at the khanda ka amrit initiation ceremony. The Mool Mantra is also the opening statement of the Guru Granth Sahib and prefaces many of its hymns, including the Japji. It defies translation. The following should be regarded as no more than paraphrase and interpretation:

Being is One, by name truth eternal; creator of all and all-pervading spirit; fearless and without enmity; timeless and formless; beyond birth and death; self-enlightened; known by the Guru's grace.

The phrases in the middle section of the Mool Mantra need not concern us very much here. They may be regarded as warnings against adopting concepts of God which suggest that he is subject to change and mood, birth and death, error and anxiety, in brief that he is like the deities of the puranas. Against this rejection of avatar is the insistence that Being is One, and that God is known by the Guru's grace. This last statement is crucial to an understanding of the concept of Guru, but it can only be examined when the first phrases have been considered.

The opening phrase, 'Being is One', found on the canopy above the Guru Granth Sahib in many gurdwaras, may be regarded as the Sikh equivalent to Om which is similarly placed above the figures of deities in Hindu temples – Ik

39

Oankar ultimately refers to the world of Hindu philosophy, to the word 'ekam' of the Rig Veda (1.164.46): 'To what is one, sages give many a title; they call it Agni, Yama, Matarisvan.' Significantly, no other name for God follows Ik Oankar, only Guru Nanak's favourite term 'Sat', Truth.

Om or Oankar is Being itself, eternal reality, for Guru Nanak. The use of the figure 1 (ik) in connection with it may be a rejection of the kind of view expressed in Mandgala Purana, that the nature of illusion (maya) is represented by the number one.[1] There may also be an implied rejection of zero, the void, sunya, an important Buddhist idea which may have had a place in the tantric cults of which the Guru was aware. More precisely, however, the phrase 'ik oankar' must be regarded as contradicting dualistic notions of the universe, whether they be expressed philosophically by such systems as samkhya, or in the everyday divorcing of religious practice from moral conduct, the division of society into different varnas and jatis and the sectarianism of religion. It was probably these practical expressions of disunity which the Guru had most in mind. In every respect God is 'one, the only one, the one without a second'.

My Master is the One, brother, and he alone exists. (AG 350)

Everything else is derived from him and has no independent existence.

The One Being [Oankar] created Brahma,
The One Being fashioned the human mind,
From the One Being emanated mountains and aeons.
The One Being created the Vedas. (Adi Granth 929)

God is liberator as well as creator.

It is through the One that the world is saved.
It is through the One that God-conscious beings are released. (AG 929)

However, God is also unknowable. First, his essence is such

1 Quoted by Alain Daniélou, *Hindu Polytheism* (Pantheon Books 1964), p. 7. For the Sikh doctrine of maya see McLeod (1968), pp. 185-7 and Cole and Sambhi (1978), pp. 82-5.

that it is beyond man's comprehension. He is devoid of all attributes; he is pure being; Being itself.

> He who unfolded the three [gunas] has made his abode in the fourth. (AG 1038)

God is beyond the three gunas. He is nirguna, devoid of attributes. This is the fourth guna to which Guru Nanak refers.

Secondly, he cannot be discovered. However diligently and sincerely one searches for God, he cannot be found. No matter now carefully men scrutinize the created universe, study sacred texts, listen to religious teachers, go on pilgrimages, practise asceticism or perform rituals, God remains unknown.

> Brahmins read books but do not understand them. They instruct others but go astray themselves, though they trade in wealth. They wander about the world speaking lies, while thou who abide by the name are blest. Many pandits and astrologers deliberate over the Vedas. They glory in disputation, argument and controversy. They continue to come and go (die and be reborn). (AG 56)

Such teachers are helpful to no one:

> A foolish man residing with a pandit hears the Vedas and shashtras but like a dog with a crooked tail he remains unchanged. (AG 990)

Worship, even apparently if it is sincere, can achieve nothing:

> Sacrifices, burnt offerings, charity given to acquire merit, austerities, even worship, are all worthless; the body continues in suffering. (AG 1127)

> God cannot be won by rites or deeds. Neither can learning help in understanding him. The four Vedas and the Puranas also have failed to reveal his mystery. (AG 155)

God cannot be understood or realized through cleverness. (AG 221) Apparently there is no hope. God is immanent, but unknowable.

For Guru Nanak this desperate paradox was broken when God revealed himself at Sultanpur. Effort, learning, seeking had met with no success, but in a moment the divine initiative had met his needs. With this in mind we can turn to the last phrase of the Mool Mantra – 'gur prasadi', 'known by the Guru's grace'.

A verse which sums up much of Guru Nanak's teaching on the subject says,

> Good actions may produce a better existence, but liberation comes only from God's grace. (AG 83)

Sikhism accepts the Hindu notion of karma to explain the nature and form of a person's present existence. Good actions procure a good birth, bad actions result in regression, but the destiny of the unenlightened is endless coming and going. The law of karma has led to a person being where he is, it can take him no further. The key to moksha is grace.

> Karma determines the nature of our birth, but it is through grace that the door of liberation is found. (AG 2)

> Nanak says, all we receive is by the grace of the Beneficent One. (AG 5)

According to the Mool Mantra this grace is imparted by, or belongs to, the Guru. It is 'gur prasadi', 'known by the Guru's grace'. Who is the Guru? Often the answers which Guru Nanak gives to this question are ambiguous. He simply uses the word 'guru' or 'gurbani', meaning Guru's word or instruction, and these might refer to himself, to some other human teacher or perhaps to God. However, he does make explicit statements:

> The Guru is God, ineffable, unsearchable. He who follows the Guru comprehends the nature of the universe. (AG 1125)

Or again, using the Vaishnavite name Hari for God, he says:

> Renounce self-centredness and pride. Serve Hari, the Guru, the Lake of Immortality, thus you will obtain honour in his court. (AG 21)

Guru Nanak taught that God is saguna, possessing qualities, as well as nirguna, without attributes. In the important composition Siddha Gosht, written in the form of a discourse with a group of yogis, he stated his belief very succinctly:

> From his absolute condition he, the Pure One, became manifest; from nirguna he became saguna. (AG 940)

To appreciate the point that Guru Nanak was making it is necessary, as usual, to recall his experience of being taken to God's court. Not only does the experience seem to have been visual but, more important, he was commissioned to 'sing God's praise', and 'to spread your glory, by singing your word'. The emphasis was not merely on meditating upon God as 'Nam' or 'Truth'; those words were to be given meaning, for Guru Nanak found himself inspired to teach and compose hymns. It is also appropriate to recollect some words from the Katha Upanishad:

> The single word announced by all the Vedas, proclaimed by all ascetic practices, in search of which men practise chastity, this word, I tell (you now) in brief, Om – this is it. (2.15)

Om is not only the name of the One Reality from whom or from which everything is derived; Om is also the primal sound which becomes articulate in the Vedas. As the Prasna Upanishad says, 'The syllable Om is Brahman . . .' The Rig Vedic verses bring him down to the world of men (Katha Upanishad 5.3). Besides using the word 'bani' or 'gurbani' for the words he received from God and uttered in the forms of hymns, Guru Nanak also used the word 'shabad' or 'gur-shabad'. Shabad, meaning 'word', is another term rich in meaning in the Hindu tradition. The shabad-brahman (or shabda-brahman) is the causal word; the cosmos is a manifested utterance of Brahman, the expression of an idea. To this may be added the importance of the mantra given by the Guru to his disciples, in many forms of Hinduism.

What Guru Nanak teaches is that nirguna Brahman becomes manifest and personal as Guru. Consequently, when the Siddhas in the discourse, Siddha Gosht, asks Guru Nanak to name his Guru, he replies:

> The word is the Guru and the mind continually (focused

43

on it) is the disciple. By dwelling on the ineffable One, I remain detached. Nanak says, God the eternal cherisher of the world is my Guru. By meditating on the unique word the ocean of existence is crossed. (AG 943)

While it may be claimed that in Guru Nanak's teachings the word guru or the term gurbani (the guru's word, instruction or teaching), refers unambiguously to God, it must be recognized that for his disciples the words of Nanak, their Guru, and the word of God were virtually indistinguishable. Though each Sikh could experience God as immanent, through grace, as Nanak himself had, for many that grace must have seemed to be bestowed by the human preceptor. There are further explicit statements that God is the Guru, perhaps intended to check popular devotion to the human gurus. For example, Guru Arjan said:

> The True Guru is God [Niranjan]. Do not believe that he is in the form of a man. (AG 895)

Such a verse might be regarded as a corrective to those bards, doubtless representative of many devotees, who wished to regard him as an avatar.

Elsewhere Guru Arjan states that his Guru is the Supreme Brahman, but he is willing also to give him sectarian names:

> My Guru is Supreme Brahman [Parabrahman], my Guru is Gobind.
> My Guru is Parabrahman, he is Bhagvan.
> My Guru is God, Allekh and Abhekh. (AG 864)

Here is a desire to express the view that all paths were included in the one Sikh path. Guru Arjan may have wished to represent Sikhism as the third way, the alternative to Hinduism and Islam. The testimony to God as Guru which began with Nanak is also reaffirmed by the last of his successors, Guru Gobind Singh.

> Know that the eternal and incarnate One is my Guru. (Chaupai)

Here he is stating that the only form which God takes is that of incarnation of himself in the believer. However, the possi-

44

bility of misunderstanding is present here as in the verses of Guru Gobind Singh.

The shift of emphasis from the word preached by the ten Gurus to the preachers may have originated in the pious devotion of the disciples to their 'Baba', a reverent affection that may be found in the disciples of Hindu gurus living today, but it must have developed with the need to provide the Panth with discipline. From the moment that Guru Nanak preferred Angad to his son Lakshmi Chand and bestowed the guruship on him, the Sikh movement was open to the possibility of divided allegiance. As the Panth grew, becoming wealthy and powerful, it became a project to be coveted. Not surprisingly, the writings of the fourth and fifth Gurus in particular emphasize loyalty and obedience. Their allusions to the guru or the gurbani may ultimately refer to God, the Guru of Gurus, but they may also point to themselves, his chosen representatives. So Guru Ram Das denounced the wilfully mistaken, those who stubbornly refused to follow the Guru:

> He who heartily adores the Guru obtains boons and his heart's desire. He who slanders the Guru, him the creator destroys. . . He who does not obey the perfect Guru's command is perverse, he is robbed by ignorance and poisoned by worldliness. . . Those who are turned Guru-wards keep aloof from such a person. They leave his company to sit near the Guru. He who does not own his Guru publicly is not a good person. The company of the saints says he loses his capital and profit. (AG 307/308)

Even the good karma which brought this man so close to liberation is lost.

The contrast between fake and true gurus and Sikhs is explicit in some other words of Guru Ram Das:

> In an attempt to emulate the true Guru some others utter filth, bad and good sermons, but because of falsehood they are soon devastated. In their heart is one thing, in their mouths quite another. They hanker after poisonous wealth and pine away for it. . . They who have deceit, wickedness and falsehood in their minds, those lepers the True Lord

45

separates away. The true Sikhs sit beside their Guru and serve him. The false ones find no place even though they search. They to whom the words of the True Guru are not agreeable, accursed are their countenances. Condemned by God they wander about. (AG 304/305)

There is probably intentional ambiguity in the use of the phrase 'True Guru'. The first time it is used it probably refers to the author himself, Guru Ram Das. The second time, God is probably meant, but when the two are placed together the reader or hearer is undoubtedly invited to recognize that God and the human Guru are essentially one.

One other observation by the fourth Guru might be mentioned, one which seems to suggest an attempt to manipulate the Panth for motives of self-interest as Prithi Chand, the Guru's eldest son, is reputed to have done.

The Guru's disciple (gursikh) shall not again draw near the one who desires to have some work done by the Sikhs without the True Guru's authority. (AG 317)

The first explicit description of the way in which a Sikh should order his daily life was also provided by Guru Ram Das:

He who calls himself a disciple of the true Guru, let him rise at an early hour, before dawn, and meditate on Nam, the all-pervading divine spirit. Let him bathe and make an effort to cleanse his mind in the inner tank of nectar. Let him repeat the name of the Lord as taught by the Guru. This will wash away the stain of sin from his mind. When the sun rises, let him sing the Guru's hymns and throughout the busy day discipline his mind to live consciously in the presence of God. He who constantly remembers God, the Lord, such a Sikh is dear to the Guru. (AG 305)

The word gurbani, the Guru's hymns, presumably now has a sectarian meaning, referring to the hymns of Guru Ram Das's predecessors, and perhaps of his own, but this famous passage is important for another reason. It combines Guru Nanak's teachings about the way in which one might grow in grace with what might be described as the institutionalizing of grace. Rising before dawn, at the time known as amrit vela, bathing and singing the gurbani are means of appropriating grace, as is the way of loyalty expressed in some words of Guru Arjan:

> The disciple who lives in the Guru's fold should submit to his will and commandment, not feeling proud of what he does. He should always meditate on the Lord's name. Truly, he who surrenders his mind to the Guru, such a servant has his desires fulfilled. He who serves without desire or reward, he alone attains the Lord. (AG 286)

Guru Nanak taught that grace is the gift of God. It cannot be earned, it is given to those upon whom God wishes to bestow it.

> As is the Lord's glance, so becomes the mortal,
> Without the Lord's gracious glance no one is saved.
> If God shows mercy, then one remembers him.
> His soul is softened and he remains in the Lord's love.
> His soul is made one with the Supreme Soul.
> His mind's duality is reabsorbed in the True Mind.
> By the Guru's grace the Lord is attained. (AG 661)

However, the bestowing of grace is only a beginning, the striking into flame of the divinity latently present in each human being. Guru Nanak taught that natural man, that is, someone who has not yet been enlightened, is characterized by haumai which might be interpreted as self-centredness or self-reliance. He believes in self-effort. He is confident that moksha can be achieved, through knowledge, the practice of yoga. Any effort, according to the Guru, is bound to failure, even the singing of devotional hymns, because no one can free himself from the round of rebirths.

> In haumai (practising self-reliance) man fails to perceive the true nature of liberation. In self-reliance there is worldly attachment and its shadow, doubt. By acting under the influence of haumai, man causes himself to be born repeatedly. If he understands haumai, he can find the door of liberation but otherwise he argues and disputes. Our karma is inscribed according to the divine will. He who

sees the nature of the divine will perceives his haumai also. (AG 466)

Haumai is a term frequently found in the Guru's writings. There is no need to give further examples. Instead, it is necessary to probe beyond haumai, which is only a characteristic, to consider the two kinds of person Guru Nanak describes. The first is 'manmukh'. 'Man' means heart, mind, soul or psyche. Natural man is manmukh, 'self-willed'. He behaves in obedience to the judgement of his own personality and consequently lives an aimless life. Sometimes he may do good, sometimes harm, like an uncontrolled elephant crashing about in a forest, but he lacks real goals and purpose.

> The man acts as the man dictates. Sometimes it expresses virtue, sometimes evil. (AG 832)

The man is intrinsically neither good nor bad.

> Within my man lurk the five (evil impulses, lust, covetousness, attachment, wrath and pride), and so like a wanderer it has no resting-place. My man has not found its resting-place in the merciful Lord, for it is caught up in the false attachments of greed, deceit, sin and hypocrisy. (AG 359)

When the man, for which the best English term may be 'personality' (that which makes us persons) has come under control, he is radically changed. Guru Nanak said, 'To conquer the man is to conquer the world' (AG 6). Duality, wrong attachment, the influence of haumai cease to worry the person who, instead of being manmukh, is gurmukh, 'God-oriented'. He is on the way to becoming God-filled. Grace produced the God-oriented person; there are certain techniques to be followed by those who seek to become gurmukh.

Guru Nanak, in common with many sants and Sufis, stressed the importance of meditating upon God's name, nam simran.

> Sacrifices, burnt offerings, charity given to acquire merit, austerities, even worship, are all worthless, and the body continues to endure suffering. Without the name of God (nam) there is no release. He who, with the Guru's help, meditates on nam (practises nam simran) finds liberation.

48

Without God's name one eats poison, speaks evil, dies meritless and so transmigrates. (AG 1127)

Nam simran, or nam japna, the practice of God remembrance, calling God to mind, is more than an act of repetition. It is an act of grafting the mind or personality (the man) on to God.

Repeating (the name) of the True God means engrafting him in the man. (AG 567)

It is a process of immersion which results in the transformation of life, so that the work begun by God in the imparting of grace is completed in a perfect human being whose every thought is of God and whose every action is directed by God. Comparing the devotee to a young girl preparing to leave her home for that of her husband, on marriage, Guru Nanak said:

Walk in the Guru's love. Meditating on the True Name you shall find bliss in the palace (of God). Meditate on the True Name and you shall find bliss. Your stay in your father's house is brief. When you go to your real home you shall know the Truth [Sat] and you shall live eternally with your Beloved. (AG 689)

Nam simran is the path by which one walks from this world to God's. Every Sikh should meditate daily, using the Japji in the morning and the Sohilla in the evening. This practice of using formal compositions is a way of attempting to ensure that nam simran does not degenerate into the meaningless utterance of a word or mantra.

'Nam' and 'Sat' are not meaningful in themselves: they represent concepts of deity which are expressed in the hymns of the Gurus. Sikhism, however, is essentially a congregational religion and another technique for developing God-consciousness so that the individual becomes gurmukh in the singing of kirtan. Kirtan, the congregational singing of bhajans, songs in praise of God, is an important aspect of bhakti Hinduism. The inspired teachers of this tradition, including the north Indian sants, conveyed their message in the form of bhajans written in the vernacular. The Sikh Gurus went further than many bhakti sants by their emphatic insistence upon belonging to the community. We have already seen that Guru Nanak established sangats wherever he went, creating the model community at Kartarpur. Guru Amar Das required the members of the Panth to assemble in his presence three times a year. One of the motives for insisting that to be a Sikh involved membership of a fellowship was the belief that if good company encourages good conduct, the assembly of men and women who had experienced the Guru's grace would stimulate spiritual development. So Guru Nanak taught:

> In the company of those in whose personalities (man) the True Lord dwells, the mortal becomes gurmukh. (AG 228)

This belief is the natural corollary of the view that God is one without a second. The Sikh who realizes this will lose his belief in individuality, which is part of a natural but unregenerative world view in perceiving the essential unity of mankind with God.

Although Guru Nanak taught that liberation or union (sahaj) with God was achieved by grace, nevertheless effort in the form of good works has its place. It is useless as an attempt to win God's favour: the Guru's benign glance falls on whomever he chooses to receive it. Nevertheless, actions are a way of serving God. They are a form of worship and can assist spiritual growth:

> Good conduct, in accordance with the Guru's instruction, is in itself worship. (AG 1343)

One of the key precepts of the Sikh faith is:

> Truth is the highest of all virtues, but higher still is truthful living. (AG 62)

The principle of honest hard work is one of the important features of Sikhism and is written into the Sikh way of life as sewa or gursewa, the service of the Guru. Guru Ram Das performed sewa for his father-in-law, Guru Amar Das, by carrying water. Frequently, acts of sewa are of a manual nature–repairing the gurdwara, cooking in the gurdwara kitchen–but they also include teaching in a gurdwara school in Britain or working in an orphanage in Armitsar. Though sewa is often specifically applied to service on behalf of the

Sikh community, strictly speaking any work performed for the benefit of mankind is sewa, for the True Guru is present in every living being.

The Path to Union with God

At the end of the Japji, Guru Nanak's most famous composition, five khands or realms are described which constitute the soul's path to union or the perfection of the 'man'. They have presented scholars with problems of etymology and interpretation,[2] but the essential clue to understanding them seems to be the recognition that they describe the ascent of the soul to God, as Terry Thomas has recently pointed out, or the journey inwards, not the movement of God towards the human soul.[3] The five khands are the realms of piety (dharam), knowledge (gian), spiritual effort (saram), grace (karam) and truth (sach). The first realm is that in which all people live. Progress through it depends on taking the law of karma seriously. The person of pious conduct may attain the second stage. The realm of knowledge is one in which the seeker after truth becomes aware of the vastness of the universe and the mystery of existence. Seized by wonder and awe he enters the realm of effort and develops the spiritual and intellectual powers of reason and perception to their limits. He has now gone as far as he can in developing his natural gifts. The realm of grace or fulfilment can be reached only with the help and assent of God. Though the bard Bhai Gurdas said,

If man goes one step towards him
The Lord comes a thousand towards man,

nevertheless the grace is not merely reward for effort. If Guru Nanak's personal experience taught him that grace comes from God, observation of life convinced him that not every seeker is successful. Often it was upon the worthless, those who had made no effort and acquired no merit, that grace fell. However, Guru Nanak was socially conservative in the

2 McLeod (1968), pp. 221-6; the issue is also fully discussed by Terry Thomas, *Sikhism: The Voice of the Guru*, Unit 12 of the Open University Course AD 208 (1978), pp. 41-6.
3 Op. cit., p. 45.

sense that he taught social responsibility. One of his reasons for preaching the householder's life as the ideal was to encourage men to remain with their families, serving God by serving their fellow human beings. Effort has spiritual and social worth, but its limits must be recognized.

> Good actions may procure a good life, but liberation comes only from his grace. (AG 2)

Consequently, forms of religion which implied that effort could win liberation received Guru Nanak's condemnation.

The realm of grace is the region where only the greatest of godly people live, the bhagats like Namdev and Ramanand, though no names are given.

> In the realm of grace spiritual power is supreme, nothing else avails. Brave strong warriors in whom the Lord's spirit lives dwell there, those who remain absorbed in praising the Lord. Their beauty defies description, the Lord lives in their hearts. They do not die and are not deceived (into a wrong perception of the world). The congregations of the blessed live there too. They dwell in bliss with the True One in their hearts. (AG 8)

Finally, the man or personality enters the region of truth where God exists in his formless state. It is completely indescribable. It can be experienced only by the liberated soul, the perfected man.

> In the realm of truth dwells the formless One who, having created, watches over his creation. He looks upon them graciously and his people are in bliss. There is world upon world, form upon form. All have their function as God's will [hukam] ordains. The Lord sees his creation and, seeing it, rejoices. To describe this (realm) is hard, hard as steel to the hand. (AG 8)

In this realm, says Guru Nanak, there are infinite places, infinite bodies and forms. The destiny of the gurmukh is not, apparently, absorption in the One but a unity which preserves some kind of distinction. Yet again we are invited perhaps to turn to Guru Nanak's experience of being taken to the divine court. There, in the realm of truth, he became aware that

God is the one and only one, the one without a second, but he experienced not absorption but standing in God's presence.

There is a sense in which Sikhism does not regard liberation (Moksha or mukti) as the highest goal. 'Heaven is wherever God's praise is sung' (AG 749), said Guru Arjan. He described as follows the person who had attained eternal bliss:

> The man who has the love of God's commands in his heart is said to be jivan mukt (liberated within the body). For him release is a present reality; joy and sorrow are both the same to him, his happiness is eternal and there is no separation from God. As is gold so is dust; as is nectar so is bitter poison. Honour and dishonour are the same. The pauper and the king are alike. He who regards success in this world as an enterprise ordained by God, is said to be liberated while in the body. (AG 275)

The emphasis in these verses is upon the here and now. Characteristically the Guru's concern is not with some post mortem existence but with the bliss which his disciples can enjoy as householders living in their villages. It is the spiritual gift which the devotee seeks from the Guru.

> Everyone longs for paradise, liberation and heaven, and rests all hope on them. Those who desire the vision of God do not seek release, they are satisfied and comforted by that sight alone. The attachment of maya is powerful, but the saints are like the duck which sits on the pond but does not get its wings wet. (AG 1324)

These words bring us back sharply to the common sight in India of a group of followers seated in front of their guru, being taught, but, more important, receiving darshan, the grace-bestowing glance of their master which transports them at that very moment to the goal they seek.

It is not surprising, therefore, to find Guru Nanak insisting that the Guru is essential, that without him there can be no sight of the divine, no attainment of bliss.

> The mind [man] of the mammon worshipper is like a male elephant. It wanders distractedly in the forest of worldly love. Under the goad of death it goes hither and thither.

By becoming filled with the Guru's teaching [gurmukh], it will find its home. Without the Guru's word the mind cannot find the resting-place. (AG 415)

But it must always be remembered that the guru of whom Nanak spoke is God, self-manifested in order to reveal himself, so that by his grace the human personality, the man, may reach the realm of truth which is its destiny. The words 'gur prasadi' in the Mool Mantra must be regarded as a testimony to this belief.

5

The Guru Granth Sahib

Theologically, Guru Nanak had always made a distinction between himself as God's bard and the message which was entrusted to him. The declaration, 'I spoke only when you, O God, inspired me to speak' (AG 566), is characteristic of his view of himself as God's messenger. There is no reason to believe that his successors differed from him in this view. However, it is possible that from the very beginning of the Sikh movement there were disciples who made no distinction between the message and its human deliverer. Passages already considered show clearly that by the time of Guru Arjan the court bards were making extravagant claims which must have echoed popular belief.

It was at this time that Guru Arjan compiled the Adi Granth, a task which was completed in 1604. It contained the compositions of his four predecessors, the writings of such Hindus and Muslims as Kabir, Namdev, Ravidas and Sheikh Farid, as well as his own immense contribution of 2218 hymns. His primary purpose was to produce an authoritative text. Despite the work of his maternal grandfather and father, versions of Sikh hymns were being circulated which distorted the originals in favour of breakaway sectarian groups. Especially, at this time, Guru Arjan's brother Prithi Chand was disputing the leadership of the Panth. Whether other motives were in the Guru's mind or not, it is difficult to say. However, the consequences of compiling the Adi Granth and installing it in the newly built Harimandir were twofold. First, he reiterated the distinction between the human Guru and the message in a visual way which must have made an impact upon his followers, especially if, as tradition asserts, he bowed before the volume as he installed it and instructed his followers to imitate his example.[1] Some might regard this story as an eighteenth-century embellishment, as well as the claim that whenever he slept in the Harimandir the Guru always lay below the level of the Adi Granth, so acknowledging its sovereignty, but certainly the compilation of the Adi Granth must have gone a long way to reinforce the importance of the hymns which Sikhs already used in worship. Sujar Rai of Batala, in 1696, wrote of the Sikhs:

> The only way of worship with them is that they read the hymns composed by their Gurus and sing them sweetly in accompaniment with musical instruments.[2]

Secondly, the compilation of the Adi Granth[3] began a process whereby the Sikhs were to become a people of the book to an extent and in a manner which is not found in any other religion.

There is little else of importance to tell about the Adi Granth in the century following. However, there are two incidents worthy of mention for the light they throw upon the importance which was already being attached to the accuracy of the text and, by implication, to the book itself. One of Guru Arjan's disciples, Bhai Banno, decided that he must have a copy of it. He therefore asked the Guru to lend it to him so that he might take it to his village, Mangat in the Gujrat district of the Punjab. Naturally, the Guru was not willing to allow this, but he eventually permitted Bhai Banno to keep it in his village for one night and no longer, during which time he could read it to other villagers. By travelling slowly, with many stops, Bhai Banno succeeded in keeping his promise and making his own copy of the book. However, he also

1 The story is recorded in Macauliffe, vol. 3, p. 65.
2 Khulastut-Twarikh, quoted Teja Singh, *Sikhism: Its Ideals and Institutions*. Orient Longman, 1964 reprint, p. 24 (note).
3 A variety of names is given to the sacred scripture of the Sikhs. Sometimes it is simply called Granth, 'collection'. After 1708, when it was invested with guruship, it became known as the Guru Granth, a term which is a constant reminder that Sikhism has only one Guru. The use of the name 'Adi Granth' preceded the compilation of the Dasam Granth by one of his followers, Bhai Mani Singh, in 1734. Clearly 'Adi' is not therefore used for purposes of contrast; it is used to assert primacy. 'Adi Granth' might be translated as 'The Primal Collection'.

included a stanza by the woman poet, Mira Bhai, at the end of Rag Maru, which Guru Arjan had crossed out, and added the rest of a verse by the bhagat Surdas to the one line which is found on page 1253 of modern copies of the Guru Granth Sahib. When Guru Arjan heard of Bhai Banno's deceit, he condemned this copy as 'bitter' in comparison with the 'sweet' authentic version, because of the corrupted text.

The second story concerns Ram Rai, the son of the seventh Guru, Har Rai. On the death of Shah Jehan the imperial succession was disputed between his sons Dara and Aurangzeb. When the latter had secured the throne he summoned the Guru, who had supported Dara, to his court. Instead, the Guru sent his son, who was kept hostage. While the young man was at the court, the Emperor's attention was brought to a verse in the Adi Granth which seemed to be critical of Islam. It read:

> The dust of a Muslim is kneaded by a potter into clay and he converts it into bricks which cry out as they burn. (Adi Granth 466)

The original context is a discussion about cremation and inhumation in which Guru Nanak expresses the view that methods of disposing of the dead are unimportant. However, since the clay of cemeteries was often regarded by potters as the best for their purposes, there was a chance that someone who had been buried might later be cremated in the kiln!

Ram Rai overcame the problem of exegesis by saying that a scribal error had replaced the word 'beiman', meaning 'faithless', with 'Musulman'. Apparently this satisfied the Emperor, but Guru Har Rai took a serious view of his son's failure to stand by the words of the Adi Granth. He refused to see his son again, saying: 'The guruship is like tiger's milk, which can be contained only in a golden cup. Only he who is ready to devote his life thereto is worthy of it. Let Ram Rai not look upon my face again.'

In 1706, during a short period of peace, Guru Gobind Singh retired to a village known then as Talwandi Sabo but now as Dam Dama ('breathing place'), where he prepared his final recension of the Adi Granth to which he had already added his father's hymns. Two years later, knowing that the wounds inflicted by two assassins were mortal, he installed the Adi Granth as guru. He took a coconut and five coins which he placed in front of the book before making obeisance to it.[4] This act had been performed with respect to their successors by all his predecessors, with the obvious exception of Guru Arjan, Guru Har Krishen and Guru Tegh Bahadur. If there is any way in which Sikhism may be described as unique within the bhakti tradition of Indian religion, it is in its elevation of a book to the status of guruship. Other groups, for example the Kabir panthis, may have written down and so retained the teachings of their founder but the gaddi of Kabir at Benares is not occupied by a book of scripture. Guru Gobind Singh's reasons for elevating the Adi Granth to the status of Guru must be linked with his creation of the Khalsa in 1699, but the more immediate reason was probably the execution of his two remaining children in 1704 and the recognition that any succession would be disputed, together with an awareness that the circumstances of the time probably required some radical new concept of leadership. Politically and socially this took the form of the Khalsa Panth, which will be discussed later. In this, it may be argued, authority for ordering the life of the Panth and temporal authority (miri) were invested. Piri, spiritual authority, belonged to the gurbani, the scripture.

However, it was only slowly that the transition from personal guruship through to corporate guruship and finally to the situation which exists today, that of guruship invested in the scripture, effectively took place. Although the authority of gurbani goes back to Guru Nanak, as we have already demonstrated, the remarkable position enjoyed by the Guru Granth Sahib coincides with the rise of the Singh Sabha, founded in Amritsar in 1873, and the acceptance by these

4 The most probable explanation given to me of the significance of the five coins and the coconut traditionally linked with the installation of the sacred book as Guru in 1708 was provided by K. S. Kathuria of Huddersfield. He suggested that the coconut represents the created universe, the hairs on it being the vegetation. The coins are the five elements of air, earth, fire, water and ether. They also represent the skill of man. Thus the world of God and man was offered to the new Guru for his protection. The gesture also acknowledged the sovereignty of the Guru. The rite itself is probably far older than Sikhism.

reformers of the use of the printing press to disseminate copies of the scripture. From this time the Sikhs became a people of the book to the degree that they are today. Copies of the book itself achieved identity of length, being of 1430 printed pages.

The term 'gurdwara' may have been in use from the time of Guru Hargobind to describe buildings for worship erected by his predecessors or set up by him on sites associated with them. Now the word is used of any place where a copy of the Guru Granth Sahib has been installed. A building owned by the Sikh community will be a gurdwara, so also will a room in a private house, if it contains the scripture. No matter where the book is installed, a number of features will be found. It will be placed on a cushion, perhaps resting on a more elaborate structure, but effectively a small string bed or stool called a manji or manji sahib. Normally, above the book will usually be a canopy, perhaps a temporary one called a chanini, made of cloth and suspended from the ceiling by strings, often a permanent one made of wood, attached to the manji by wooden posts.

The position of the Guru Granth Sahib in a building is determined by the belief that it should occupy the most exalted position. In a two-storey house the gurdwara will therefore be in an upstairs room. If the house has an attic (in the case of the kind of house gurdwaras Sikhs first used in Britain) and the attic is considered for some reason unsuitable, it will be kept closed so that no one may accidentally walk above the book. In the room where the Guru Granth Sahib is installed, it will be raised above the congregation – who will sit on the floor – often by being placed on a platform. The complete structure containing the scripture is called a palki, akin to the word palanquin, or takht, meaning 'throne'. The principle of literally giving the Guru Granth Sahib exalted status is also seen in the practice of carrying it on the head by a bearer who takes it to the manji sahib from a room where it may have been kept for the night, or by someone who takes a copy on foot from a gurdwara to a private house in a Punjabi village. When an act of worship is in progress the book will have an attendant. Seated behind the manji the attendant holds a chauri made of peacock feathers or yak or nylon hairs embedded in a wooden or silver handle.

The place of the Guru Granth Sahib in a room is determined by two practical considerations. First, at weddings those standing should circumambulate it. Therefore it needs to be placed far enough away from any wall for this to be comfortably possible. Second, no one's back should ever be turned on the book, so it would be inappropriate for the entrance to the room to be in a position which made this (unintentionally) a possibility. Often the Guru Granth Sahib will be installed at the end of the room opposite the door. There is no theological requirement that the book should be set at the Amritsar-facing end of the room, for example. The scripture itself is the focus, not some compass point or geographical location in India or elsewhere.

A few comments upon the significance of the Guru Granth Sahib in the gurdwara, and its treatment, might be appropriate at this point. It is enthroned and treated as, for example, Guru Nanak is depicted in portraits: he is shown seated on a gaddi with a tree above his head acting as a chattri or canopy, with Bhai Bala in attendance holding a chauri of peacock feathers. However, the seat of the scripture is called a manji sahib, not a gaddi, and no copy of the scripture anywhere in the world is accorded more respect than any others. Sometimes concern has been expressed that the treatment of the scripture is so excessively reverential that it amounts to idol worship. In some gurdwaras the book is carried each night from the room where worship takes place to another room, to be literally put to bed. Some Sikhs have declared their thankfulness that the copy of the scriptures which Guru Gobind Singh installed as Guru was destroyed in the Vada Ghallughara, or great massacre, of 5 February 1762. Otherwise, they argue, it would have become to Sikhism a focus of worship and a place of pilgrimage, rather like Kabir's wooden sandals at the Kabir Chaura in Benares. The sandals are daily washed and the charn armrit is given to devotees.

Certain practices attached to the Guru Granth Sahib which do not seem consistent with the teaching of Sikhism have occasionally crept into Sikh devotionalism. There is the practice of putting the scripture to bed, like a statue of Krishna or some other Hindu deity, which has already been mentioned. Sometimes a jug of water is placed near the Guru

Granth Sahib in a gurdwara; and when the book is carried in the open air someone may walk ahead of it sprinkling the ground with water. These are essentially Hindu practices for warding off evil. In the same category may be placed formalized akhand paths. These are continuous, unbroken readings of the Guru Granth Sahib conducted by relays of readers. They last for about forty-eight hours. Such readings often precede a wedding or are ways of celebrating an important religious occasion, for example a gurpurb, the anniversary of a Guru's birth or death. Reading the scripture can be an occasion of considerable spiritual refreshment and comfort. This is especially true of the sidharan path, or broken reading, which lasts ten days and may be undertaken by families after a bereavement. However, the practice has developed for groups to be formed which spend much of their time conducting akhand paths, with the emphasis shifting from the spiritual nourishment gained by hearing the gurbani to the automatic power to remove pollution as a result of reading it.

At this point, of course, we are entering the difficult, not to say dangerous, area of trespassing upon the devotee's private motives and interpreting the meaning of his actions. Concepts of pollution may be in the thoughts of some Sikhs when they remove their shoes before coming into the presence of the Guru Granth Sahib. This must surely have been true of those who rebuked a visitor, in my presence, for carrying his shoes through the gurdwara. Others will merely appeal to custom, while many will rationalize by explaining that dirty shoes should not come in contact with carpets which people are going to sit on. The same variety of reasons can be given for bathing before entering a gurdwara. But whatever the motives, those who come before the book and especially those who handle its pages should not only take off their shoes, they should have bathed fully.

The actions of a person approaching the Guru Granth Sahib combine practices analogous to the respect given to gurus, to worship in a Hindu temple and the respect given to a secular prince. The worshipper bows or prostrates himself in front of the book until his forehead touches the ground and makes an offering of money (though flowers or food may be given) before sitting on the floor in front of the manji sahib.

61

Before leaving he will receive karah parshad, a warm sweet pudding made of flour or semolina, sugar, water and ghee. Bowing, touching the feet of the rupa of a Hindu deity, offering money, receiving prasad (Punjabi parshad) from the priest, are all aspects of puja. Even the canopy over the Guru Granth Sahib bearing the symbol ੧ੳ, Ik Oankar, is similar to that over Hindu statues bearing the symbol ॐ, Om. The resemblance is so strong that it is impossible to deny with certainty a Hindu influence. Seeing the congregation standing for Ardas encourages one to press the comparison further, for it is very reminiscent of the Arti ceremony which is often performed before a guru. But it is interesting and important to note that prayers, not arti, are offered in the presence of the Guru Granth Sahib.

Diwan is the name given to Sikh congregational worship. It is also the word for the place where a Mughal emperor held court, or the name given to the act of holding court and giving audience. Chauris like the one used in the gurdwara can be seen in picture of Mughal emperors or in portraits showing the return of Prince Rama to Ayodha. In the latter, the Prince's wife Sita and his brother Lakshman are shown holding an umbrella over his head and a chauri of peacock feathers.

The most appropriate comparison to make with the behaviour of a Sikh entering a gurdwara is that of a disciple approaching the guru. The disciple comes into the guru's presence bringing a gift, dakshina. He bows or prostrates himself, he kisses or touches the guru's feet, he receives prasad. At a spiritual level he seeks and receives darshan and in some circumstances shaktipat. These are the benefits obtained by the Sikh who takes part in congregational worship. For many Sikhs the very sight of the scripture is a means of receiving grace. Though they should join in the singing of kirtan, many will prefer to listen even when they know the words. Being in the Guru's presence and listening to the sound of the gurbani is clearly in itself a rich spiritual experience, of the kind one observes in watching Hindu disciples seated in front of their gurus. Sometimes shaktipat, the transfer of spiritual power, can be received in a physical form, when the worshipper receives a romalla from the Guru

Granth Sahib. This is a cotton or silk covering which Sikhs sometimes provide for the scripture. It may be given at any time, but the receiving of one seems to be confined to certain occasions – perhaps a marriage, more often before undertaking a journey, or at a bereavement. The romalla may be regarded as auspicious in itself or may be accepted as a token of the sangat's good wishes or concern.

As the scripture became the Guru of the Sikh community and the focus of worship, so it naturally assumed a significant place in the domestic rites of passage and initiation into the Khalsa. A child is named by opening the scripture at random, turning to the first hymn on the left-hand page and taking the first letter of the first word. Sikh marriages are considered valid when they have been conducted in the presence of the Guru Granth Sahib. In some communities of the Sikh diaspora, where the law requires marriages to be registered, the custom is sometimes found of a registry office wedding being held in the town where the bride lives, followed by a gurdwara wedding there some months later. The couple would not be regarded as man and wife, or even allowed to meet unchaperoned, until the gurdwara ceremony had taken place. Even though some gurdwaras are now registered for the solemnization of marriage, this practice does not seem to be diminishing, perhaps because it gives purpose to a formal meeting of the two families at the groom's home. Although a corpse is not carried into the presence of the Guru Granth Sahib, perhaps because of lingering notions of pollution, the Suhi, a hymn of Ravidas found in the Adi Granth, is often recited by those in the funeral procession. When the body has been cremated, it is usual for the family to arrange a sidharan path which should be completed on the tenth day.

When Guru Gobind Singh founded the Khalsa in 1699 he instituted a new form of initiation, khande-ka-pahul or khande-di-pahul, also known as amrit pahul. These names are used interchangeably for the amrit sanskar. Charn amrit and charn pahul, literally foot-bleaching, had been the early Sikh method of initiation. This was performed by drinking water that had been poured over the guru's feet. The change is mentioned in the story of Rattan Rai, an Assamese prince who became a follower of the tenth Guru before the Khalsa

63

was formed and so received charn pahul, and in the words of the son of a Sikh named Manula who said, 'I am the son of Manula. We are both initiated Sikhs. My father became a Sikh by charn-pahul while I was initiated by the double-edged sword (khande-di-pahul).' There is no need to describe the new form of initiation here, apart from saying that it is performed by five male Khalsa Sikhs in the presence of the Guru Granth Sahib.

The final act of a Sikh congregation, at diwan, is to ask the Guru for guidance. This is done by opening the Guru Granth Sahib at random and reading the first complete passage on the left-hand page. The same custom is observed in the home, either informally by using a gutka, the small collection of hymns which most families or individuals possess, or by ceremonially opening the Guru Granth Sahib and reading from it after first taking a bath. Tradition asserts that 'vak lao', to give the practice its Sikh name, developed in the eighteenth century when scattered groups sought the guru's guidance or instruction. Literally, vak lao means 'take a command'. Usually the impact of putting oneself at the command of the word of the Guru is not remarkable enough for comment but there is on record one extremely important instance which illustrates what obedience to the word can entail.

The year 1920 was the time of mass movement when large numbers of Punjabi outcastes were seeking to improve their social status by accepting Christian baptism or initiation into the Khalsa. For Sikhism these mass conversions were not always wholly welcome for they affected the balance and cohesion of the Panth. Close family ties with Hindus and the social status of those who associated with men and women who were still regarded by Hindus as outcastes, posed problems. Commensality was the most sensitive area, for by eating with outcastes those of higher social and hierarchical groups suffer pollution and must be regarded as outcastes by conservative Hindus. There were of course many Sikhs, especially some of the Singh Sabha reformers, who, remembering the opposition of the Gurus to caste discrimination, supported the full acceptance of these converts into the Khalsa. In 1920, after a mass amrit ceremony in Amritsar, the converts naturally wished to make their pilgrimage to the Golden Temple to offer karah parshad. Encouraged by some reformers they stood their ground while conservatives opposed them knowing that many Sikhs would refuse to eat the karah parshad which they had provided. At last it was agreed that the Guru should be consulted and his command obeyed. The scripture was opened at random. From it these words were read:

> Upon the worthless he bestows his grace, brother, if they will serve the True Guru. Exalted is the service of the True Guru, brother, to hold in remembrance the divine name. God himself offers grace and mystic union. We are meritless transgressors, brother, yet the True Guru has drawn us to that blissful union. (AG 638)

It was accepted that 'worthless' and 'meritless transgressors' (the word can be used of criminals) referred to the outcaste converts. In fact these words spoken by Guru Amar Das appropriately described the spiritual effect of their conversion and initiation. They were therefore allowed to offer karah parshad.

Sikhs are not given to personal testimonies, but there are many members of the faith and congregations who devoutly attempt to live their lives according to the teachings of the Guru Granth Sahib. As one hears a Punjabi woman singing the Sohilla in the garden as evening falls, or sits with a family of mourners being consoled by words of scripture, one is aware of men and women who, through the ministry of the Adi Granth, have found the living Guru within themselves and have experienced the truth of the words which Guru Arjan wrote at the end of the Adi Granth in a passage called 'Mandavani':

> In the platter are placed three things, truth, contentment and meditation. The nectar name of the Lord, the support of all, has also been put therein. If someone eats this food, if someone relishes it, he is emancipated. This cannot be forsaken, so keep it always enshrined in your mind [man]. Falling down at the Lord's feet the dark world ocean is crossed. Nanak says, everything is an extension of the Lord. (AG 1429)

Beyond and underlying the apparent formalism of Sikh worship is a devotional dimension which the non-Sikh observer can scarcely perceive. It is fed by the private practice of nam simran.

6

The Guru Panth

In 1699 the tenth leader of the Sikhs, known then as Guru Gobind Rai, summoned his followers to Anandpur for the Baisakhi assembly. For some time issues of morale and leadership had been causing him anxiety. The system of delegating authority to the massands was now proving unsatisfactory. The Guru had no confidence in them, as two of his Swayyas, numbers 29 and 30, show:

If anyone serve the massands, they will say,
'Fetch and give us all thy offerings.
Go at once and make a present to us of whatever property there is in thy house.
Think on us day and night, and mention not others even by mistake.'
If they hear of anyone giving, they run to him even at night; they are not at all pleased at not receiving.

They [the massands] put oil in their eyes to make people believe that they are shedding tears.
If they see any of their own worshippers wealthy, they serve up sacred food and feed him with it.
If they see him without wealth, they give him nothing, though he beg for it; they will not even show him their faces.
Those beasts plunder men, and never sing the praises of the Supreme Being.

The plan devised by the Guru to infuse a spirit of strength and unity in his followers was put into effect at the Baisakhi assembly. At the height of the fair he emerged from his tent. With drawn sword he demanded the head of a Sikh. No one stepped forward from the silent, aghast crowd. The demand was repeated. One loyal Sikh, Daya Ram, a kshatriya, came forward and was led to the Guru's tent. A thud was heard, then the Guru reappeared alone, his sword dripping blood, to repeat his demand. Dharam Das, a Jat, offered himself and followed the Guru to the tent. Three more times the request was made. Mukham Chand, a washerman, Himmat Rai, a water carrier and a barber, Sahib Chand, in turn obeyed their leader's command. When the fifth blow had been heard the Guru drew back the tent flap. The men stood unharmed. Beside them lay the bodies of five goats.[1] The Guru then addressed the astonished crowd, but no reliable record of his words survives.

The Sikh tradition given by Macauliffe[2] mentions a number

---

1 The events of Baisakhi 1699 cannot be narrated with any certainty. It is impossible to be sure of what Guru Gobind Singh said or did. There is agreement, however, on a number of points:
  i that the Baisakhi assembly of 1699 was one of unparalleled significance;
  ii the names of the panj pyares;
  iii that a new body, the Khalsa, was the lasting consequence of the occasion;
  iv that the rite of initiation by the sword (khande ka pahul) replaced that of foot initiation (charn pahul).
Discussion by recent Sikh scholars sometimes indicates a concern with issues of morality, the unnecessary killing of five goats, or the miracle of raising five men to life, rather than with an attempt to reconstruct the historical event. Two examples are Kartar Singh, *Life of Guru Gobind Singh* (Lahore Book Shop, Ludhiana 1951), p. 140 and Sahib Singh, *Life History of Guru Gobind Singh* (Raj Publishers, Jullundar 1967), p. 81. Sometimes speakers at Baisakhi gatherings or at initiation ceremonies suggest that what actually happened inside the Guru's tent or enclosure always remained a secret between him and the panj pyares. This would justify the view of some Sikhs that only members of the Khalsa should witness the amrit ceremony.
    The description given by Kartar Singh which expresses the view that the Khalsa is the embodiment of the Guru, is sometimes portrayed visually: there are pictures showing the Guru and the panj pyares not only dressed alike but with identical physical features.
    For a careful Sikh analysis of Baisakhi 1699 see J. S. Grewal and S. S. Bal, *Guru Gobind Singh*, Punjab University (Chandigarh 1967), especially Appendix C.
2 Macauliffe, vol. 5, pp. 93–7. Apparently Macauliffe believed that the Tawarikh-i-Punjab of Gulam Muhai-ul-Din contained an eyewitness report of the Anandpur assembly, whereas it was written in 1848. Any

of other significant details. It states that the Guru dressed the five men in splendid raiment so that they shone like the sun. He said to them:

> My brothers, you are in my form and I am in yours. He who thinks that there is any difference between us errs exceedingly.

When he had invited the five men to sit near him, he addressed the whole assembly:

> In the time of Guru Nanak there was found one devout Sikh, namely Guru Angad. In my time there are found five Sikhs totally devoted to the Guru. These shall lay anew the foundation of Sikhism and the true religion shall become current and famous throughout the world.

Then, prostrating themselves before the five, the assembly said:

> Hail to the Sikh religion! You, brethren, have established it on a permanent basis. Had we offered our heads like you, we too should be blessed.

Next, the Guru took some sugar crystals which he dissolved in water contained in an iron bowl, by stirring them with a double-edged sword. As he stirred the water with the khanda he recited the Japji of Guru Nanak, the Jap which he had composed, the Anand of Guru Amar Das and some of his own swayyas and Chaupai. He then gave the five men five palmfuls of the amrit to drink, sprinkled it five times on their hair and eyes, and commanded them to repeat the words,

'Waheguru ji ka Khalsa
Waheguru ji ki fateh.'

The Khalsa are the chosen of God,
Victory be to our God.

2 *cont.* sources used by Muhai-ul-Din in describing the incident have not been traced. Through Macauliffe, Tawarikh-i-Punjab has been the basis of later accounts: for example, Khushwant Singh (1977), vol. 1, p. 84 and I. Banerjee, *Evolution of the Khalsa*, vol. 2 (Amukherjee, 3rd edn 1972), pp. 108–25.

The Guru himself requested the five hesitant men, famed in Sikh history as the panj pyares, or beloved five, to administer amrit to him. His words were:

> I am the son of the Immortal God. It is by his order that I have been born and have established this form of initiation. They who accept it shall henceforth be known as the Khalsa. The Khalsa is the Guru and the Guru is the Khalsa. There is no difference between you and me. As Guru Nanak seated Guru Angad on the throne, so I have made you also a Guru. Wherefore administer the amrit to me without hesitation.

A disciplinary code was then laid upon the Khalsa. The Guru said that they should believe in one God upon whose name they should meditate daily, rising before dawn to use the prescribed hymns of the gurus. They should abandon the old scriptures (for many these would be the Puranas rather than the Vedas, but the phrase is applied comprehensively to the Hindu scriptures and to the Qur'an or Bible for Muslim and Christian converts). They should not worship Hindu gods and goddesses; in particular, belief in avatars should be rejected. They should not make pilgrimages. Drinking alcohol, taking drugs and smoking were prohibited as were fornication, sexual relations with Muslim women, entering into marriage with families who practised female infanticide, eating meat slaughtered according to Muslim rites, and cutting the hair. Five symbols were to be worn, known as the five Ks, for each begins with that letter in Punjabi. These were uncut hair, a comb, a steel wristlet worn on the right hand, a short sword and a particular form of trousers. (To these the turban is added, so constituting the 'uniform' of the male Khalsa Sikh.) Members of the Khalsa should keep themselves fit, as warriors. The Guru also said that those men who became members of the Khalsa should take the name Singh, meaning 'lion' and women the name Kaur, meaning 'princess'. This was to emphasize and facilitate the repudiation of caste distinction which was also part of the disciplinary code. The Guru himself set the example and consequently is known to history as Guru Gobind Singh, not Gobind Rai.

When these conditions of membership were proclaimed to

the gathered assembly, many, especially brahmins and ksha-triyas, withdrew but some 80,000 Sikhs followed the panj pyares and their Guru in receiving initiation into this new fellowship. The word Khalsa is itself significant. Its derivation is sometimes traced to the Arabic word khalis, meaning 'pure', but it is said to be related to the Mughal use of the word Khalsa to refer to land in the emperor's personal pos-session. A hukam nama or edict of Guru Tegh Bahadur referred to the sangat of Patan as the Guru's Khalsa.[3] One of Guru Hargobind's edicts described the sangat of 'the east' as his Khalsa. This means that these groups were directly linked with the Gurus rather than through the allegiance of massands.

Finally, it is said that while Guru Gobind Singh was defin-ing the purpose of this new form of initiation, two sparrows dipped their beaks into the nectar. When they had drunk some of the liquid they flew off, confronted a hawk and killed it in combat. This originated the Sikh proverb, 'Through entering the Khalsa, sparrows become hawks.' This story should not be regarded as referring to some quality present in the amrit, but to the will and determination to fight for dharma of those who have taken amrit.

This anecdote certainly points to one of Guru Gobind Singh's reasons for creating the new institution. It was to inspire his followers by giving them a sense of dignity and respect. They were now to consider themselves rajputs or kshatriyas. This was further effected by sanctioning, one might even say sanctifying, arms, together with the provision of a strict code of discipline. Altogether this amounted to giving the Sikhs a sense of pride which has never diminished over the centuries, ideals of valour tinged with chivalry, but more immediately personal allegiance to their young Guru, for at the time he was only thirty-two.

There have been other consequences. One is the final emergence of Sikhism as a distinct movement with political as well as religious ideals. Despite the three annual gatherings introduced by Guru Amar Das, the compilation of the Adi Granth in 1604 and its permanent display in the Harimandir

3 J. S. Grewal and S. S. Bal, op.cit., p. 226, note 26.

where people could go to check its contents, in practical terms the Sikh movement must still have been somewhat incoherent. Besides a core of men and women faithful to the Gurus, there must have been a large number of nominal Sikhs some of whom were more followers of the massands than disciples of the Gurus. The foundation of the Khalsa provided Sikhism with the distinctiveness which even the casual observer can easily perceive today. The penalty for becoming distinct was that Sikhism also became sectarian, requiring of its members certain observances which could from time to time obscure the ideals of Guru Nanak rather than complement them. Sometimes, it must be said, the debate about who is a Sikh has therefore centred upon uncut hair, the turban, or whether a Sikh could run a shop selling alcoholic drinks or cigarettes, rather than defining him as one who has been enlightened and is becoming gurmukh through God's grace, the practice of nam simran and living honestly according to the teachings of the Sikh scriptures. In this, of course, Sikhism is not unique. There are also important reasons, which the historian and the sociologist of religion will appreciate, for a continued emphasis upon the symbols, the outward form and code of discipline associated with the Khalsa.

It would be easy to conclude, sometimes from Sikhs' own pride in the exploits of the Khalsa, that its purpose and function was purely military. However, it should be noted that the Khalsa code of discipline required complete adherence to the ideals of Sikhism. Depending on the circumstances the teachings have been upheld in different ways. Sometimes the means has been that of the use of outward force, but at others, for example in the late nineteenth century, as we shall see, it has been through the development of educational institutions.

Mention has already been made of political ideals which the foundation of the Khalsa stimulated. Of course, these had already existed for nearly a century before 1699. Since the time of Guru Hargobind's small army the Sikh movement had been a potential threat, however minor at first, to Mughal authority. It could become the focus of north Indian unrest and did, at least to some extent, under the ninth and tenth Gurus. In the eighteenth century the challenge to Mughal rule intensified. With it came the slogan, 'Raj karega Khalsa', 'The Khalsa shall rule'. It might be argued that the high point of these political aspirations was reached in the period 1799 to 1839 during which Ranjit Singh, leader of one of the Sikh armies, conquered the Punjab and established an independent Sikh state. Paradoxically, however, he was also responsible for transforming his province into what might today be described as a secular state by employing Hindu, Muslim and western advisers. In fact, in 1809 he deprived the Sarbat Khalsa, the assembly of all Khalsa leaders or members, of the right to make political decisions. In future gurmatta, Khalsa decisions (literally, the word means 'the mind or intention of the guru') were to be confined to issues of doctrine and other religious matters. The idea of the Guru Panth is explicit in some words ascribed to Guru Gobind Singh:

Where there are five, there am I,
Where the five meet, they are the holiest of the holy.

Through initiation any five Khalsa members formed a group in which the Guru was mystically present. The initiation of Guru Gobind Singh into the Khalsa by the panj pyares which symbolically absorbed guruship into the Panth is apparently unparalleled in the history of religion, but within Sikhism it may be regarded as the culmination of a process which began with Guru Nanak's installation of the disciple Lehna as his successor, Guru Angad. Not only have we such statements as that of the bards, who said that Guru Nanak put his light (joti) into Angad (Adi Granth 966), but Sikh tradition contains a number of more explicit sayings such as:

The Baba is not in the samadh, he is in the heart of Angad,

and to take the development further,

The Baba is also in the holy congregation.

Another popular saying asserts,

The Guru is twenty carat, but the sangat is twenty-one carat.

These statements assert that guruship achieves completeness

in the unity of the guru with his disciples. Bhai Gurdas took the idea even further:

> One is a Sikh, two is a sangat; where five are, God is there. (Var 13.19)

There had been ample precedent for these popular appraisals of the Guru–Sikh relationship in the words of the early gurus themselves. For example, Guru Nanak wrote:

> Friends have come to my home. The True Lord has brought about my association with them. When it pleased the Lord, he caused me to meet them. I have obtained bliss by meeting the saints. I have obtained the very thing that my mind longed for. Day and night my heart is enraptured through meeting the saints. (Adi Granth 764)

The context of these words does not support the view that Guru Nanak may have been thinking of Namdev, Kabir or other sants. The holy company seems to be the fellowship of human beings. Here, in verses which the bridegroom's party sings as it approaches the bride's house, is early literary evidence for the importance which Guru Nanak attached to the sangat. For Guru Nanak the aphorism that good company encourages good conduct was true. He said:

> Man becomes good in good company, he pursues virtue and cleanses himself of vice. (AG 414)

But the value of the sangat was more than moral, it was spiritual:

> The company of those who cherish the Lord within themselves, turns mortals into holy beings [gurmukh]. (AG 228)

In the hymns of Guru Arjan considerable prominence is given to the sangat. Perhaps because he was confronted with rivalry and opposition, he recognized the importance of strengthening the guru–chela bond. In the following passage the Guru explores a variety of dimensions of the relationship. Though the word translated 'saints' is santan, there is no reason for thinking that the reference is to the hymns of such sants as Kabir or Namdev. A more vital and personal relationship seems to concern the Guru, who must be extolling the sangat.

74

I am the dust of the saints' feet and I seek their protection. The saints are my powerful support and the saints are my ornaments. I have now befriended the saints. I have obtained what was preordained for me. I have surrendered my heart to the saints. My dealings are with the saints, my business is with them ... By the saints' grace I have attained the supreme bliss and obtained peace. Nanak says, My soul is reconciled with God and is entranced in God's love. (AG 614)

Perhaps the most significant idea in these lines is that of the saints being the source of grace through whom the Guru became entranced in the Lord's love. It must be remembered that his father and grandfather were gurus. It should also be noted that Guru Arjan was the first guru to have been born into a Sikh household. All his predecessors came from Hindu families.

Rather than cite other examples,[4] we shall note the words 'protection' and 'surrendered' in the passage quoted above. Sikhism is an extremely democratic religion. It has no priesthood; women as well as men may be among its office-holders and often have been. The statement of humility, 'I am the dust of the saints' feet', was no mere verbal formula, as the following two examples show. Guru Arjan was seeking a suitable marriage for his son, Hargobind. The possibility of arranging for his son to marry Sada Kaur, the daughter of Chandu, Akbar's finance minister, seemed in many ways to be an attractive proposition. Discussions therefore began. A priest and barber, the traditional match-maker in Indian society, saw the young man and encouraged Chandu to permit the marriage. He, however, believed that such a liaison with a poorer family of lower social status would not be advantageous. To make matters worse, the Guru did not even behave like a khatri. He ate with anyone, practising some new religion rather than Hinduism. Nevertheless, persuaded by his wife, Chandu gave his consent. The Sikhs of Delhi who had learned of the plans and of Chandu's feelings, sent representatives to the Guru before the barber could return to

4 A few other examples are AG 201, 496 (known as the birthday hymn because it is generally sung on birthdays), 749 and 764.

complete the contract. They told him that Chandu had said that for his family the marriage would be like taking a brick from an upper storey and dropping it into the gutter, and they asked the Guru to reject the proposal. The Guru accepted their advice and so avoided the mistake he was in danger of making.[5]

The other story concerns Guru Gobind Singh. Sometime after the formation of the Khalsa, the Guru and a small force of Sikhs were besieged at Chamkaur. There was no chance of their being relieved or breaking through the Mughal lines, though it might be possible for some to escape if the rest could create a diversion. Guru Gobind Singh declared his intention of dying with his men. However, they held a council which ordered him to attempt to leave Chamkaur to reach the bulk of the Sikh army in order to continue the struggle. He accepted their decision as being that of the Khalsa of which he was only one member.[6]

After the death of Guru Gobind Singh in 1708, leadership of the Sikhs passed to one of the Guru's officers whose given name was Lachman Das but who preferred to call himself Banda, slave of the guru. He has passed into history as Banda Singh or Banda Bahadur, Banda the brave, as a tribute to his heroic struggle against the Emperor Bahadur Shah. Although Guru Gobind Singh had been with the armies of the Emperor in 1708, and his life cannot be described as an incessant struggle against Mughal rule, nevertheless he died having failed to persuade the Emperor to punish Wazir Khan,

5 Macauliffe, vol. 3, pp. 70–80 gives the story in greater detail and includes the view that the Guru would have avoided the error even without the guidance of his followers.
6 In Macauliffe's account (vol. 5, p. 189) it is said that the Guru circumambulated five Sikhs three times before he left Chamkaur and entrusted the guruship to them with the words: 'Wherever there are five Sikhs I shall be in their midst.'
   Teja Singh, *Growth of Responsibility in Sikhism*, p. 55 describes an incident which occurred as Guru Gobind Singh passed the shrine of the saint Dadu. The Guru lowered the weapon he was carrying, as a sign of respect. Knowing this to be contrary to Sikh teachings, his followers challenged his action and imposed on him a fine of 150 rupees. Teja Singh says that the Guru did this to test his disciples by seeing whether they would follow his example or the precepts of the Sikh faith.

governor of Sirhind, who had ordered the execution of his remaining sons, Zorawar Singh, aged nine, and Fateh Singh, aged seven. Banda Singh therefore decided to take justice into his own hands. In 1710 his army confronted Wazir Khan, who was defeated and killed. Sirhind was captured. Bahadur Shah decided that the Sikhs should be suppressed. During the next five years a fierce struggle ensued in the Punjab culminating in the defeat, capture and execution of Banda Singh, in March 1716, with many of his followers.

Although Banda is an heroic figure in Sikh history, his stature is less than it might have been because he attempted to continue the line of the gurus by having the title conferred upon himself.[7] Long before his defeat many Khalsa members had ceased to support him. Against his claims to represent Sikhism arose the cry:

'Raj karega Khalsa',
The Khalsa shall rule.

It was made clear that guruship was now corporate in the Khalsa and that anyone who assumed leadership did so through its consent and maintained his position only as long as he enjoyed its approval. The spirit was one which might be described as democratically republican. The political climate was one of tension and strife. From the Sikh point of view the eighteenth century was an almost continuous struggle for survival. In these circumstances the corporate aspect of guruship, represented by the Khalsa, was of greater importance than the concept of scriptural guruship, though it was the latter which finally became dominant. Eventually the corporate principle lapsed. It should be noted that the Panth never possessed the authority to formulate doctrine contrary to the teachings of the Adi Granth. In this respect the scripture has always been the successor of the ten gurus.

The execution of Banda Singh was followed by Mughal attempts to suppress their Sikh subjects. The Sikh community's response was to organize itself into small fighting units called jathas, each under the leadership of a jathedar, who was appointed by the entire assembled Khalsa, known as the

7 Macauliffe, vol. 5, pp. 249–50.

Sarbat Khalsa. This body continued the custom established by the gurus and assembled twice yearly, at Baisakhi and, for Diwali, at Amritsar. Besides appointing jathedars it also passed resolutions known as gurmattas, decrees of the guru, which were considered binding upon all Khalsa Sikhs. It must have been impossible for the Sarbat Khalsa to assemble every year and at length the practice of the entire Khalsa meeting together gave way to that of gatherings of the jathedars. Eventually the jathas brought together in the Dal Khalsa the Khalsa army which was itself divided into twelve misls. The word misl means 'like',[8] implying that the divisions were equal. However, some of these fighting groups were considerably larger than others. Though one could join any of the units, choice was often determined by family connections, jati, or the geographical area in which the misl was based. The jathas of former times were merged into the misls and their leaders were replaced in the Sarbat Khalsa by the new misldars often known as sardars (chieftains).

The misls, though notionally divisions of one Dal Khalsa, seldom fought in one army and enjoyed considerable independence under their misldars. However, between 1747 and 1769 the Afghans launched no fewer than nine invasions of the Punjab in an effort to replace waning Mughal control with their own authority. These invasions and the ability of men like Jassa Singh, misldar of the Ahluwalia misl and supreme commander of the army, maintained unity in the Khalsa. Their survival, followed by victories against the Mughals, encouraged the belief in an independent Sikh state. This hope was realized by Ranjit Singh, the outstandingly able leader of the Sukerchakia misl. Far from founding a democratic republic rule by the Sarbat Khalsa according to the teaching of Sikhism, however, Ranjit Singh established himself as maharaja of an autocracy. Though an effigy of Guru Nanak, not his own, was struck on coins, his court was known as the Darbar Khalsaji and government was said to be Sarkar Khalsaji, the rule of the Khalsa. Before long he began to see Hindu, Muslim and European advisers. In 1809

8 The Persian word 'misl' also means 'file'. A record of each jatha's exploit was carefully filed. Sometimes it is suggested that this meaning of misl explains the choice of the word as a name for the Sikh regiments.

he ended the right of the Sarbat Khalsa to pass political gurmatta. The modernization of his army and a centralized government left no place for the misls and the threat to authority which they represented. It would be an exaggeration to say that Ranjit Singh rose to power because of the aspirations of the Sikhs summed up in the slogan, 'Raj karega Khalsa'. It was only when they were threatened that the Sikhs were united. At other times they often quarrelled and fought among themselves. It would be true, nevertheless, to say that he made use of the ideal to justify his ambition, but it was his ability which enabled him to establish a kingdom where other Sikhs had failed. On the other hand it is correct to hold him responsible for ending not only meetings of the Sarbat Khalsa but also the realization of Sarkar Khalsa, Khalsa Rule. After the Maharaja's death in 1839, the Punjab state was soon annexed by the British. A century later the Sikh dream in the form of a republic within the British Commonwealth was revived but hopes were more than dashed when the homeland of the Sikhs was divided between Pakistan and India. The reorganization of the Punjab province of India in 1966, with the formation of the Punjabi Suba, has gone some way towards meeting Sikh demands for Home Rule, but for many Sikhs the future they envisage lies in maintaining political influence and control in the Punjabi Suba, and acquiring as much influence as possible in the government of India. These are, however, to be regarded as the aspirations of an important minority group rather than a desire to reassert the guruship of the Khalsa.

Before leaving the institution of the Sarbat Khalsa it might be interesting to consider the description which Sir John Malcolm gave of a gathering which took place in 1805. Though he called it a Guru-mata, a name sometimes used by other Sikhs,[9] it is a meeting of the Sarbat Khalsa which is being portrayed.

When a Guru-mata, or great national council, is called, as it always is, or ought to be, when any imminent danger threatens the country, or any large expedition is to be undertaken, all the Sikh chiefs assemble at Amritsar. The

9 It is used in this sense by Teja Singh, *Sikh Ideals and Institutions*, p. 44.

assembly, which is called the Guru-mata, is convened by the Acalis; and when the chiefs meet upon this solemn occasion, it is concluded that all private animosities cease and that every man sacrifices his personal feelings at the shrine of the general good; and, actuated by principles of pure patriotism, thinks of nothing but the interests of the religion and commonwealth to which he belongs.

When the chiefs and principal leaders are seated, the Adi Granth and Dasam Padshah ka Granth are placed before them. They all bend their heads before these scriptures and exclaim, 'Wa! Guruji ka Khalsa! Wa! Guruji ki Fateh!' A great quantity of cakes made of wheat, butter and sugar are then placed before the volumes of the sacred writings, and covered with a cloth. These holy cakes, which are in commemoration of the injunction of Nanac [sic], to eat and to give to others to eat, next receive the salutations of the assembly, who then rise and the Acalis pray aloud, while the musicians plays. The Acalis, when the prayers are finished, desire the council to be seated. They sit down, and the cakes being uncovered, are eaten of by all classes of Sikhs: those distinctions of original tribes, which are on other occasions kept up, being on the occasion laid aside, in token of their general and complete union in one cause. The Acalis then exclaim: 'Sirdars (chiefs)! this is a Guru-mata!' on which prayers are again said aloud. The chiefs, after this, sit closer and say to each other: 'The sacred Granth is betwixt us, let us swear by our scripture to forget all internal disputes and to be united.' This moment of religious fervour and ardent patriotism is taken to reconcile all animosities. They then proceed to consider the danger with which they are threatened, to settle the best plans for averting it, and to choose the generals who are to lead their armies against the common enemy. The first Guru-mata was assembled by Gur Govind; and the latest was called in 1805, when the British army pursued Holkar into the Punjab.[10]

The description may be an idealized one to some extent. It is doubtful whether the reconciliation of all animosities was

10 Quoted in McLeod (1976), pp. 48–9.

as easily achieved as the passage suggests. However, there is the suggestion that an over-riding unity should persist in the gathering. Even more important is the mention which Malcolm makes of the presence of the Adi Granth and Dasam Granth before which each member of the assembly bowed, thus acknowledging the guruship of the scripture. Clearly it was in the mystical presence of the guru, represented by the sacred books, that the Sarbat Khalsa met. Perceiving in the cakes karah parshad, which is also made of wheat (often in the form of semolina), butter and sugar, it is easy to imagine oneself in a gurdwara taking part in a normal Sikh service.

Not every Khalsa Sikh was caught up in the wars of the eighteenth century. Many others raised their families, tilled their land and kept the faith without being members of the Khalsa or giving sons to the jathas or misls. Often men belonging to these groups of Sikhs were called sahajdharis, a name sometimes used in an unkindly manner to describe those who have not taken amrit and who are 'slowly' adopting the Sikh way of life. The word 'sahaj' in the compound itself may refer to gradualness or, perhaps more properly, to Guru Nanak's use of this term to describe the ecstasy experienced through nam simran. Sometimes so-called sahajdharis prefer to call themselves Nanak panthis. To some extent their importance in the Sikh tradition is perhaps that they represent an aspect of Sikhism which has not sanctioned the use of military force; but probably more significant in their fidelity to the scripture. No attempt is being made to create an antithesis between keshdari as militaristic and sahajdhari as pious. Such a contrast would be a gross distortion of reality. Furthermore, today devotion to the Guru Granth Sahib is equal among Sikhs whether they wear the turban or not.

What is being suggested is that the recounted military exploits of the eighteenth century may serve to obscure the persistence of local sangats whose devotionalism was kept alive and nourished by the Guru Granth Sahib. In the nineteenth century, when the Punjab had been annexed by the British, it was expected that Sikhism would disappear in the vast ocean of Hinduism. The importance of the Khalsa had gone. The Sarbat Khalsa and the concept of corporate guruship were memories. Sikhism apparently meant no more than a form of Punjabi nationalism associated with a long-dead leader, Guru Gobind Singh. Among the reasons for its survival must have been the continuity of corporate worship based on the sangat, a tradition going back as far as Guru Nanak himself.

When the revival of the Khalsa took place, it was in response to the threat to Sikhism posed by Christian missions, and more particularly the Arya Samaj. In 1834, before the collapse of Sikh independence, an American Presbyterian had arrived in the Punjab. From his work developed the Ludhiana Mission. After the annexation British officials encouraged missionary activity, which grew so much that one is given the impression of innumerable denominational organizations competing with one another for converts.[11] When Maharaja Dalip Singh became a Christian in 1853, a Christian school was established in Amritsar, and fears that Sikhism was threatened more from Christianity than Hinduism became considerable. However, the principal danger was reversion into Hinduism. Perhaps at the height of Sikh fortunes under Ranjit Singh the Sikhs were only a sixth of the Punjab's population at most. Intermarriage with Hindus was common among the Nanak panthis who, lacking the external symbols of the Khalsa and not bound by their codes of discipline, lacked distinctive cultural attributes of their own. Many gurdwaras, it seems, had passed into the ownership of Hindu families. Besides the Guru Granth Sahib they housed statues and pictures of Hindu deities. Non-Sikh practices had crept into Sikh worship. Paradoxically, however, it was the Hindu renaissance which terminated this period of reabsorption by provoking the Sikhs to assert that they were not Hindus – largely through the revival of the Khalsa as a force for religious renewal.

In 1877 Swami Dayanand Saraswati, founder of the Hindu reform movement known as the Arya Samaj, came to the Punjab where both Hindus and Sikhs acclaimed him. He appeared to personify a Hindu renaissance which could answer the criticisms made by Christianity, by purifying Hinduism of social and ritual distortions which found no

---

11 Khushwant Singh (1977), vol. 2, p. 137 provides a list.

justification in the Vedas. Much of what the Arya Samaj stood for seemed to be present in the teachings of the gurus. Not surprisingly, some Sikhs were ready to see in Dayanand a champion against the Christian threat. However, it soon became clear that his insistence on the infallibility of the Vedas left little place for the Guru Granth Sahib. It was claimed that Dayanand had dismissed Guru Nanak as a hypocrite (dambhi). Sikh leaders found themselves allied with Muslims and Christians in demanding that his book, Satyarth Prakash, should be suppressed as it contained material which was offensive to the three faiths.

A more lasting consequence of the Arya Samaj presence in the Punjab was the formation of Singh Subhas, Sikh organizations dedicated to promoting religious and social reform, largely through education. They saw that the hope of Sikhism lay in purging the Panth of Hindu influences. The way to success was through reviving the Khalsa ideas, expressed through loyalty to the Guru, the provision of a code of discipline which would define Sikh beliefs and practices, regaining control of gurdwaras and setting up Sikh educational institutions. This was made possible by the growing economic prosperity of the Punjab. The readiness of the British to allow Sikhs who joined the army to retain the Khalsa symbols also encouraged the cause of Sikh identity. The improvement in Sikh fortunes can be judged from the increasing number of outcastes who sought amrit initiation. However, it was not until 1925 that the Punjab government approved the Sikh Gurdwaras Act, which vested control of many gurdwaras in the province in the hands of a committee mostly elected by Sikhs, the Shromani Gurdwara Parbandhak Committee. Earlier, in 1909, the Anand Marriage Act was passed which legalized the Sikh form of wedding and made a further contribution to freeing Sikhism from Hindu practices. Again the focus was the Guru Granth Sahib.

The story of this chapter is that alongside the importance of the human gurus and the bani which they uttered grew a significant belief in the sangat as a community of godly people. This was strengthened in 1699 when Guru Gobind Singh vested guruship in the newly created Khalsa. During the eighteenth century it was the Sarbat Khalsa which was the effective guru of the Sikhs but with the success of Maharaja Ranjit Singh, representative of the Sarbat Khalsa, paradoxically the concept of corporate guruship passed into obscurity. When, in the late nineteenth century, a revival of the Khalsa ideal took place, the notion of corporate guruship was not revived. Instead, the Khalsa became the institution of initiated Sikhs dedicated to defending and enhancing the guruship of the scripture.

7

The Present Situation

We have seen that the term 'guru', as applied in Sikhism, has a number of meanings. It refers to the manifest form which God takes as preceptor of mankind so that he may be described as Sat Guru. It may also be applied to the ten human guides through whom the Sat Guru spoke. Consequently it is logical to describe the volume in which the message entrusted to them had been recorded, as the Guru Granth Sahib. Finally, the title guru may also be ascribed to the Panth which grew up in response to those teachings and exists to obey them and witness to them.

The composite meaning of guruship is still apparent today and the person of Guru Nanak is as deeply revered by Sikhs as it ever was. There are few homes or gurdwaras in which his portrait may not be found. He is a source of inspiration and pious devotion now as he was nearly 500 years ago. The memory of the Guru is kept alive through the janam sakhis. These are accounts of his ministry which came into existence during the century after his death. Probably during Guru Nanak's own lifetime, those Sikhs who could not be physically present with him at Kartarpur used anecdotes to re-create his presence. After his death and as the Sikh movement became more geographically widespread, the need to preserve him alive in the community would be considerably increased. The janam sakhis met that need. One of them expressed it thus:

> He who reads or hears this sakhi shall attain to the supreme rapture. He who hears, sings or reads this sakhi shall find his highest desire fulfilled, for through it he shall meet Guru Baba Nanak. He who with love sings of the glory of Baba

85

Nanak or gives ear to it shall attain joy ineffable in all that he does in this life, and in the life to come salvation.[1]

As another janam sakhi put it,

He who from the depths of his being reads this testimony will find salvation. Of this there is no doubt.[2]

During the seventeenth century in particular, when the guruship was often in dispute, the janam sakhis, centred as they were upon the unrivalled leader of the movement, must have provided cohesion. However, as the first passage quoted suggests, their primary purpose may have been that of giving darshan. Those who heard and believed beheld Guru Nanak as surely as those who lived with him at Kartarpur. The janam sakhis are still used by Sikhs, not only by scholars who attempt to construct biographies from them, but by the pious who desire to be transported from the gurdwara where their stories are told to foster devotion or illustrate the meaning of one of the guru's hymns, to the Guru's real presence. However, darshan is obtained not from the janam sakhis but from the Guru Granth Sahib. The point is perhaps made by the proscription of bowing before a picture of Guru Nanak or one of his successors. A Sikh should bow only towards the Guru Granth Sahib; to prevent any ambiguity, portraits of the Gurus should not be placed near the scriptures. Originally the intention may have been to prevent such portraits from being used like the rupas of Hindu deities. The effect has been to reinforce the guruship of the Adi Granth.

The respect accorded to Guru Nanak in the janam sakhis has scarcely been diminished over the centuries. Sikh children will point to his portrait with the words, 'He is my God'. Sikh writers reiterate the teachings of the janam sakhis that Guru Nanak's birth was non-karmic, so that he was born already perfect. This view is sometimes to be found in writings by Sikh theologians. It is fully expressed in *Sikhism: Its Ideals and Institutions* by the famous Sikh scholar Principal Teja Singh

1 McLeod (1980), p. 11.
2 Ibid., p. 241.

– a book which is widely used within the Panth as a work of reference.[3] He writes:

> The Sikh Gurus were perfect, and are described as such in the Sikh scriptures. Guru Nanak himself says in *Sri Rag:* 'Everybody else is subject to error; only the Guru and God are without error.' (AG 61) And Guru Arjan says in *Bhairon:* 'Whoever is seen is defective: without any defect is the true Guru, the Yogi.' (AG 1140) The state of perfection attained by the gurus is lucidly described in the eighth and eighteenth cantos of Guru Arjan's *Sukhmani*. The same Guru says in Asa:

> God does not die, nor do I fear death.
> He does not perish, nor do I grieve.
> He is not poor, nor do I have hunger.
> He has no pain, nor have I any trouble.
> There is no destroyer but God,
> Who is my life and who gives me life.
> He has no bond, nor have I got any.
> He has no entanglement, nor have I any care.
> As He is stainless, so am I free from stain.
> As He is happy, so am I always rejoicing.
> He has no anxiety, nor have I any concern.
> As He is not defiled, so am I not polluted.
> As He has no craving, so do I covet nothing.
> He is pure, and I too match Him in this.
> I am nothing: He alone is everything.
> All around is the same He.
> Nanak, the Guru has destroyed all my superstitions and defects,
> And I have become uniformly one with Him. (Adi Granth 391).

> The Guru is sinless. In order, however, to be really effective in saving man, he must not be above man's capacity to imitate, as he would be if were a supernatural being. His humanity must be real and not feigned. He should have a nature subject to the same laws as operate in the ordinary

3 Teja Singh, *Sikhism: Its Ideals and Institutions*, 2nd edn 1964, reprint pp. 18–19.

87

human nature, and should have attained his perfection through the same Grace as is available to all men and through perfect obedience to God's Will. The Sikh Gurus had fought against sin and had overcome it. Some of them had lived for a long time in error, until Grace touched them and they were perfected through a constant discipline of knowledge, love and experience in the association of their Gurus. When they had been completely attuned to the Will divine and were sanctified as Gurus, there remained no defect in them and they became perfect and holy. Thereafter sins did come to tempt them, but they never gave way and were always able to overcome them. It is only thus that they became perfect exemplars of men and transformed those who came under their influence to veritable angelic beings.

Teja Singh begins with an appeal to scripture. However, he clearly accepts the view that the word 'Guru' in the passage he quotes refers to Guru Nanak. In this he is adopting a fairly common position but one which can cause some confusion. Throughout the hymn from which Teja Singh has quoted, the necessity of the Guru is emphasized, but Nanak is not to be regarded as speaking of himself. He is alluding to the importance of grace and asserting that unless God manifests himself, man's plight is helpless. Ritual bathing, pilgrimages, reading the scriptures or joining religious orders, all these forms of religion are ineffective.

The verses by Guru Arjan quoted by Teja Singh need not, of course, support a view that the human Guru was born perfect. The last two lines suggest that the spiritual unity to which the rest of the quotation refers has resulted from a growth in grace which Sikhism argues may be enjoyed by anyone. Teja Singh himself accepts this view in stating that 'When they had been completely attuned to the Will divine and were sanctified as Gurus, there remained no defect in them and they became perfect and holy'. Such an interpretation accords with Hindu teachings about fully enlightened beings acquiring no further karma; perhaps it owes more to the bards and janam sakhis than it does to the Sikh preceptors themselves. It may also represent a natural desire within the

Panth to revere a founder figure. One cannot help surmising that Teja Singh is eager to portray Guru Nanak as a Sikh equivalent to Jesus, perhaps responding to the influence of Christian missionaries in the characteristically Indian way of discovering within his own traditions those elements which the evangelists claimed to be distinctively or uniquely Christian.

The late Professor Taran Singh in a recent article entitled 'The Nature of Guruship in the Guru Granth' states that the Supreme Being is the Guru. He is consciousness or Jnana supreme whose chosen channel for communicating this to humanity is guruship. Taran Singh continues:

> To be communicable, the Supreme Being chooses one of his created men to be his vehicle and speak to humanity through that chosen vehicle in a language that man can understand. 'He places himself in the Guru', the specially chosen form, says Guru Nanak. He places himself as the 'light' ('jot') in the chosen man. He inspires his soul and conduct. Again, Guru Nanak, addressing a devotee, Bhai Lalo, says, 'I broadcast the jnana or knowledge as it is transmitted to me by the Supreme Master himself.' Guru Nanak's successors also said the same thing. They only proclaimed what was inspired in their holy beings by the Master as a command or communication. The voice thus received was recorded in human language and it, so preserved, became the eternal Guru. The voice 'vibrates in the pages of the Guru Granth'.[4]

A few lines further on he states:

> The Sikh Gurus have taken considerable pains to emphasize the point that the Bani, and not the body, is the Guru. But the confusion among the Sikhs does persist in practice. The 'word' or 'voice' embodied is erringly worshipped in the form of the Granth (Book). The doctrine does not allow this worship.[5]

Taran Singh's stricture might be applied to those, in effect,

4 'The Nature of Guruship in the Guru Granth' in *The Nature of Guruship*, edited by Clarence O. Mcmullen (ISPCK 1976), pp. 27–8.
5 Ibid., p. 28.

who ascribe divine or at least superhuman qualities of sin-
lessness, perfection or omniscience to the ten gurus, but it
directly refers to those who attach undue reverence to the
physical form of the scriptures. What he has in mind is perhaps demonstrated by these words of Bhai Sahib Ardaman
Singh who writes:

> We are becoming plain and blatant Book worshippers.
> They have started at some places to wrap the Holy Granth
> in warm clothes during winter and switch on the fan in the
> summer. They draw curtains around the Guru Granth
> Sahib and place parshad inside so that it can feed in pri-
> vacy. They even lull the Holy Volume to sleep by placing
> it on swinging beds. Thanks, Sat Guru, they have not yet
> started to bath the Holy Book; though at some places
> toothpicks and a jug of water are placed under it at night
> . . . The Sat guru has left no stone unturned to save us
> from such heresies (as Book worship). Of all other things
> the Holy Volume which was present at Nanded is no longer
> traceable. If it had been available we would have become
> confirmed Book worshippers long ago. Its disappearance is
> an obvious mercy that the Sat guru has taken on us![6]

He concludes his invective by reminding his fellow Sikhs that
it is the 'gurshabad', not the book or the Khalsa, which is
'the reigning Guru among the Sikhs'.

The Sikh religious community is particularly fortunate in
having in its possession the manuscript of the original Adi
Granth; it is held by the Sodhis of Kartarpur in the district
Jullundur. Some years ago, according to Dr Loehlin, it was
proposed that a photographic copy of this text should be
made, partly to ensure that scholarship would not suffer
should the disaster of destruction ever befall it, but also to
make it widely available to scholars interested in textual issues. The idea had to be abandoned because of a strong body
of Sikh opinion which saw this as tantamount to photograph-
ing the body of their Guru.[7]

Those religions which possess a scripture face two dangers.

6 *The Spokesman Weekly*, twenty-third annual number (1974), pp. 19–21.
7 M. Juergensmeyer and N. Gerald Barrier (eds.), *Sikh Studies* (Berkeley
    1979), p. 117.

90

First, there is that to which Christianity has often succumbed. In affirming that it is the spirit, not the letter, of the Bible which is important, it may claim to have liberated the text from Hebrew or Greek, making it available to almost everyone in the world in his own mother tongue. However, there has been a tendency to treat the Bible in an extremely casual manner, compared with the care which Jews, Muslims and Sikhs lavish upon their holy books. Against the danger of regarding the scripture like any other book, to be written in, or put on the shelf next to novels or gardening books, there is the second threat of bibliolatry. The Sikh scriptures are more open to this than any others, not just because they are the focus of every devotional act in a Sikh's life but because of this unique position implied in the title 'Guru'. Despite Taran Singh's protestation that it is the bani or gurshabad which is the Guru, nevertheless the name of the book, the frequency of usage and decorum in handling or even approaching the book under the possiblility of reverence becoming worship, are what the Panth must always have in the mind. Given these circumstances it may seem remarkable that in the nineteenth century the Panth agreed to printed copies being produced and used in public worship, and a little surprising not only that translations have been permitted and lately encouraged, but that these have been used occasionally in gurdwaras in England.[8] No English version has yet been installed as Guru Granth Sahib but English forms of particular hymns have been used. As communities in the Sikh diaspora, distanced from the Punjab, become unfamiliar with the gurmukhi of the scriptures, further developments are likely to take place, but here one is looking some thirty years ahead at least. However, one of the very few beneficial consequences of Britain's increasingly tight control of the immigration of people popularly classed as coloured will be the prevention of gyanis and granthis as well as imams and Hindu priests from being brought into Britain to serve their communities. As a result these will be ministered to by spiritual

8 In 1889 when the first printed edition appeared in five volumes, an injunction was issued and displayed in public places against binding them in one cover. Presumably the aim was to prevent the printed form being installed as Guru.

leaders who understand the context in which they are working. If the hope of Christianity in Africa and Asia depends on the growth of the indigenous churches, the same may be said of those faiths which have left their traditional homelands to settle in the europeanized areas of the world.

The Khalsa regards itself as the protector or guarantor of the Sikh tradition. This is especially true in the diaspora, particularly in Britain, where the world's largest Sikh community outside India is very concerned about issues of identity. Behind the right to wear the turban at work, successfully contested in Wolverhampton, Manchester and Leeds, and now generally accepted, and the legal exemption of Sikh motorcyclists from wearing crash helmets, lies the anxiety that decline in mother-tongue fluency, with the general pressures of British society, will lead to the disappearance of Sikhism. What the Christian missionaries failed to do in the Punjab, western secularism may succeed in accomplishing in Europe, America, New Zealand and finally in India itself. The Singh Sabha movement resisted the threat a century ago very largely through educational reforms. At present the elders of Britain's gurdwaras seem to hope that wearing the five Ks and the turban will safeguard their youth from deserting the faith. In India the difficulties appear to be less severe. The traditional response linked with political acumen seems to be more than adequate to the present situation.

Authority is a matter which is likely to exercise the minds of the Sikhs in the next generation. Theologically it is vested in the Guru Granth Sahib, where it is likely to remain. In practical terms issues are dealt with locally by democratically elected gurdwara committees. These are autonomous bodies capable of responding to almost any issue which faces them. However, there is also a central authority which may decide upon major matters affecting the Panth. This is a body comprising the jathedars of four major gurdwaras in India, known as takhts, literally 'thrones'. Three of these are at the gurdwaras of Keshgarh in Anandpur, Patna and Nander in the Deccan. Each is associated with an incident in Guru Gobind Singh's life, the founding of the Khalsa, his places of birth and death respectively. Each also covers a distinct part of India, thus providing a regional centre for settling disputes about the correctness of ritual. The fourth centre, at the Akal Takht, Amritsar served a political as well as religious function. It was there that the Sarbat Khalsa met until it was abandoned by Maharaja Ranjit Singh. The jathdars of the four takhts now constitute the body which pronounces upon disputes. Its decisions in the form of hukamnamas are binding upon the Panth.

This arrangement seems perfectly effective and satisfactory. However, it is quite naturally constituted to meet Indian needs. One wonders whether the Sikhs might one day reconstitute the Sarbat Khalsa, comprising representatives of the worldwide Sikh community, and place authority in its hands. Such reorganization might become necessary if and when the Sikh Panth ceases to be Punjab oriented during the twenty-first century. The doctrine of the Guru Panth is available, waiting to be revived to meet this need.

One of Taran Singh's observations on the subject of guruship has already been mentioned. We must now turn to two of his earlier articles in which he reflects upon the nature of guruship. In 1966 *The Sikh Courier* commissioned a series of articles to celebrate the tercentenary of Guru Gobind Singh's birth. Naturally, the Khalsa dominated the thoughts of many of the writers, including Taran Singh. His study is remarkable for its lack of eulogy and sectarianism but even more significant for his doctrine of the Khalsa. He begins by asserting that there are no privileged people, or lands, and no superior faiths and beliefs as such. The Wonderful Lord is an equalizing factor in the world.[9]

That there is one Universal Spirit who belongs to all people, whatever their colour, caste, country or religion, is his theme. It leads him to an enlarged, all-embracing concept of the Khalsa, summed up in the following passage:

> The doctrine of the Khalsa or the Universal Brotherhood of the Pure, proceeds from the doctrine of the all-pervasive and indivisible ultimate Reality. The Wonderful Lord manifests himself in a wonderful drama or Vachitar Natak of the cosmos and creation. In fact all the actors in this cosmic play are Khalsa or Pure; they are all saints and no sinners;

9 *The Sikh Courier*, vol. 4, no. 3, p. 29.

all are devas and not daitas – just as in the staged drama, all the actors are equals and friends, but are playing various roles which are sometimes honourable and complimentary, and sometimes contemptible and sinful. . . All sinners are also saints in the making – surely they are to be redeemed, sooner or later. So the brotherhood of the Pure is the brotherhood of the entire humanity.

When he turns his attention to the Khalsa as a body of initiated Sikhs, he describes them as

the culminating point of the Gurmat and Gurdarshan. It is an ideal society of mankind which consists of the philosophers, the Brahmgyanis, Gurmukhs, or Sikhs. It is a society of humanity so that they might transform the world into the Kingdom of Heaven.

The keshas, the turban and the five Ks which characterize the Sikh Khalsa are not to be rejected, nor are they to be regarded as perpetuating sectarianism. They are to be seen as symbolizing the ideal of universal brotherhood.

The symbol of the keshas, which every soldier of the fraternity of the Khalsa is ordained to carry is the insignia, standard and flag to symbolize these ideals.

Writing in a volume published in 1969 to celebrate the quincentenary of Guru Nanak's birth, Taran Singh expressed the view he had given of the Khalsa with regard to guruship:

The term Guru does not imply the Sikh Guru or saints of a particular area of time only; rather it indicates a divine institution or the eternal spark of the divine light which continuously and eternally shines, in the form of the divine word, in different localities at different times, to inspire men and to guide their destiny.[10]

He then proceeds to consider the terms gurmat (the path shown by the Guru) and the gurdarshan (the vision of reality experienced by the Guru). Neither of these, he asserts, must be interpreted in a sectarian manner. Naturally, the question

10 *Guru Nanak* (1969), p. 54.

94

arises, 'What then was the contribution of the Sikh Gurus?'
Having asked it, Taran Singh offers this reply:

> The Sikh Gurus once again helped the sun of dharma to
> rise. In such an attempt, they naturally simplified, crystal-
> lized and chiselled the form of dharma and gave the divine
> Light a new lustre and shape. Gurmat is the same eternal
> divine lamp, lighted by God himself and reinforced again
> and again by saints and Gurus as willed by him.

Professor Taran Singh's interpretation of guruship is shared
by Professor S. S. Kohli in a book written to present in a
clear, straightforward manner the principles of the Sikh faith.
Kohli begins by stressing the importance of the guru both in
India and in the Adi Granth, describing him as 'perfect being'
and 'the pivot of Sikh thought'. Then he raises the question
of human guruship and provides the following answer:

> In the primal age, the Guru Soul was identical with Brah-
> man. This shows that first and foremost the Guru is God
> himself. Guru Nanak and Guru Gobind Singh talk of him
> as their Guru. When the universe was created by Brahman,
> the Guru Soul pervaded the world as Ishvara, but when
> Ishvara became manifest through an Enlightened Soul in
> a physical form it adopted different names at different
> times. These enlightened souls through whom the word of
> God or Name spread in the Universe were called Gurus.
> The ten Gurus of the Sikhs are the manifestation of the
> Guru Soul. All the contributors of the Adi Granth experi-
> enced the manifestation of the Guru Soul within them.
> Since the scripture contains the message of the Guru Soul,
> his word, or Bani, it was given the status of a Guru by
> Guru Gobind Singh. The physical form disappeared with
> the tenth Guru and the Guru Soul manifested itself in the
> form of Word, Name or Bani. In fact the body is prone to
> death, but the Word lives on for ever.[11]

It may be argued that both Taran Singh and S. S. Kholi
are representing the spirit of their age, that of an India eager
to give respect to its constituent religions but equally con-

11 S. S. Kohli, *Outlines of Sikh Thought* (New Delhi 1966), pp. 90–1.

cerned to discourage sectarianism leading to communalism. They also present an interpretation of guruship which is attractive to the increasing number of people interested in interfaith dialogue. However, their view also accords with that of the Adi Granth. One would wish to say that its overall stance is against sectarianism. One of the reasons why mullahs, brahmin priests or yogis are censured is because they proclaim their path rather than God's involving people in matters of religious practice which deflect them from the truth. God's path lies beyond the religious, though Guru Nanak does not seem to deny that it may be reached through them.

Particular passages may be cited which invite this conclusion. It is an underlying theme of the Japji. Also it is found explicitly stated in these famous words:

> There are six systems, their teachers are six, and six their doctrines. But the teacher of teachers is but one Lord, though he has various vestures. (AG 12)

In some verses on pages 222 and 223 of the Adi Granth, Guru Nanak discusses some of the consequences of receiving diksha from the Guru. They include recognizing that he alone is the door to moksha, realizing that he alone exists, permeating man and woman as well as earth and sky, and acknowledging that through his grace comes all understanding and to him goes all devotion. In a passage which is notably lacking in any criticisms of yogis, he says:

> The yogi meditates on the fearless and pure Lord. Night and day he remains awake and embraces affection for the True Name. Such a yogi is pleasing to my mind. The snare of death he burns with the Lord's fire. He sheds fear of old age and death and stills his ego. He himself swims across and saves his ancestors too. He who serves the True Guru becomes a yogi. He who remains immersed in the Lord's fear becomes fearless. As is the one he serves, so does he himself become. (AG 223)

In Dakhni Oankar, a hymn that might be described as Guru Nanak's reflection upon Om, for that is what Oankar is, the

Guru praises the creative activity and self-revelation of God as Guru beginning with these words:

> It is the one Lord who created Brahma.
> It is the one Lord who fashioned the human mind.
> It is from the one Lord that mountains and ages have emanated.
> It is the one Lord who created the Vedas. (AG 929/930)

Finally, on pages 140 and 141 of the Adi Granth there are many references to the 'True Muslim'. Among them occur these words:

> By mere word of mouth one does not go to Paradise. Deliverance comes only from putting truth into practice. (AG 141)

The same transcending of sectarianism may be found in 'Vachitar Natak', Guru Gobind Singh's autobiographical poem. True, this may be read as a pæan of Sikh triumphalism for it catalogues the failure of Brahma, Siva, Vishnu, Siddhas, Saddhus, Gorakhnath, Ramanand and others to overcome formalism and successfully proclaim the path of Truth before it then describes God's command to the perfected Guru Gobind Singh, meditating on Mount Hemkunt, absorbed in the Immortal One. However, it does this in such a way as to admit that these were man commissioned by God to proclaim his Name. Thus we read:

> Muhammad was ordained King of Arabia by the Lord, but he taught the sunna to his devotees. He caused his own name to be repeated. No one fixed the True Name in men's hearts. So the Immortal One said to me, 'I have glorified you as my son, I have created you to proclaim the Panth'; go spread the faith there and restrain people from folly.' I stood up, made obeisance, and said, 'This Panth will spread in the world when thou givest assistance.'
> For this reason the Lord sent me. Then I took birth and came into the world. What he spoke, that I speak, and I bear no enmity to anyone. Those who call me Parmeshar shall fall into the pit of hell. Know me only as his slave, – and have not the least doubt of that. I am the Slave of the

Supreme Being, and have come to behold the spectacle of the world. What the Lord told me, that I tell the world, and I will not remain silent through fear of mortals. (vv. 29–33)

These verses may be read as a poem to encourage Sikhs during a time of persecution. They obviously misrepresent Islam, using words about the Prophet which Muslims would find offensive, just as they distort Hinduism, asserting that all have gone astray. However, it is what they say about the Panth that is of greatest, permanent importance. The Sikh community was not called into existence to be another sectarian movement. It was created to witness to truth by living according to the eternal and universal dharma proclaimed in the Kalyug by the Gurus. It is to this doctrine of guruship that Taran Singh recalls the Panth in his writings.[12]

We must now bring this survey of the distinctive and central concept of Sikhism to a close. It has many strands which intertwine to give strength and variety, but there are times when one dominates the other in a manner which might appear detrimental to the concept of enriching and strengthening, depending on the viewpoint of the observer and the circumstances of the Panth. The doctrine, though firmly rooted in the teachings of Guru Nanak, is dynamic and capable of further evolution. Nothing in this study which has examined it piece by piece should be allowed to detract from the richness and vitality of the whole.

Naturally the doctrine of Guru, in common with many other aspects of the Sikh faith, owes much to its Hindu parent. To witness the ways in which disciples manifest respect for their spiritual guides and to observe the relationship of Sikhs to the Guru Granth Sahib which have been described in detail in Chapter 5, is to note many similarities. However, Sikhism has been remarkably successful in resisting the temptation to deify its leaders or to perpetuate the line of human Gurus. The word 'deify' might appear inappropriate in the context of an Indian religious tradition which often regards the atman

12 A similar universal view is expressed by P. S. Sambhi, 'A Sikh Looks at the Christian Church', in *Expository Times*, July 1977.

or jiva as indestructible, eternal and essentially one with Brahman. However, it may be seen to have some value if the negative statement is made that Sikhism has resisted pressure to regard its ten teachers as avatars. The principal single reason for this success must be the care which the Gurus themselves took to point beyond themselves to God who, manifesting himself as Guru, revealed himself to mankind through words entrusted to Guru Nanak and his successors.

It must be admitted that the achievement of the ten Gurus in checking the enthusiasm of their followers has not always been emulated by the Panth within which there has sometimes been a tendency to pay more attention to the Guru Granth Sahib as a physical object than to its teaching. Some of the rules contained in the Rehat Maryada, a guide to the Sikh way of life, refer to this. This brief document, drawn up in 1945, was based upon earlier codes of conduct. It reflects very strongly the influence of the Singh Sabha movement of the late nineteenth century, though codes of discipline were in existence a century earlier. It describes a Sikhism breaking from Hindu influence. For example, ghee lamps and the ceremonial use of joss sticks are forbidden as well as the placing of a dish of water near the Guru Granth Sahib to ward off evil. The very fact that these are mentioned indicates that some Sikhs were treating the Guru Granth Sahib as Hindus did the statues of Rama, Krishna or Siva, adopting practices which Sikhs regarded as idolatrous. These warnings have not prevented bowls or glasses of water from being put near the sacred book, or water being sprinkled in its path whenever it is carried in procession or even taken from its overnight resting-place to the manji in the gurdwara. More insidious, perhaps, is the recourse to akhand paths, not in order to listen to the gurbani but because of a belief that the very practice of reading the Adi Granth from beginning to end is auspicious. Instead of reinforcing respect for the message it can encourage the notion that the book is a charm to ward off evil.

Besides the possibliity of regarding the Gurus and the Guru Granth Sahib in ways of which the Gurus themselves would not have approved, there is a danger of the Khalsa appearing as the pure Sikhs, an elitist or separatist group within the

Panth. Some Khalsa members would want to go as far as declaring themselves to be the Panth and to demonstrate this by refusing to eat food which had not been prepared by amritdhari Sikhs, for fear of pollution.

Sikhism, like other movements political, social or religious, operates in three dimensions which merge in practice to become the living faith. First, there is the realm of popular religion in which the Gurus become avatars and the book a murti or rupa. Because the Panth has always operated in the dominant cultural context of its parent it has always been inclined to revert to the ways of Hinduism which its founders rejected. Secondly, there is a level at which Sikhism functions as a sectarian movement. History has encouraged this especially the often tragic story of Sikh–Muslim relations both in the eighteenth century and during the independence struggle only a generation ago. The search for identity which is solved by wearing the turban and keshas can further foster this sectarianism. Finally, there is the Gurus' vision of a truth which transcends varna and jati, bibliolatry or the claims of Hinduism and Islam. This, as we have seen, is being re-expressed by theologians but the ideal also permeates popular and sectarian Sikhism in the theoretical emphasis upon the equality of men and women, the recognition that caste distinctions should not be observed within the Panth, and the general outgoing nature of Sikhs which can overcome traditional attitudes to Hinduism and Islam.

The concept of guruship lies at the heart of Sikhism. The human Gurus, then the Guru Panth and finally the Guru Granth Sahib have made the religion what it is. But these have always addressed themselves to external influences, for the Sikhs have seldom enjoyed the possible luxury of being able to ignore the world in which they exist. Wherever they have been they have lived as a minority. The issues with which Sikhism will have to concern itself in the future will also come from outside. They are secularism, both in India and the western world, and the consequences of being regarded as one of the world's important living religions. The response to both is likely to be found yet again in a reappraisal of the concept of the Guru.

Glossary

ad (Adi)	first, original
akal	timeless, a term used to describe God, sometimes used as a name of God
Akal Takht	literally, the Throne of the Timeless One. Originally the Amritsar palace of Guru Hargobind, its builder; now one of the four seats of the Sikh spiritual authority, the others being at Anandpur Sahib, Patna Sahib and Nanded. Its custodian (jathedar) is an employee of the Shiromani Gurdwara Parbandhak Committee. The main feature of the Akal Takht is a throne three times higher than the Mughal throne balcony in the Red Fort at Delhi, a symbol of Sikh sovereignty
akali	literally, a worshipper of the Timeless God. Used of the Sikhs of Banda Singh Bahadur who, after 1708, worked for the overthrow of the Mughals. Custodians of the Akal Takht who did not recognize the authority of the Maharaja Ranjit Singh. Since 1922 a movement dedicated to the recovery of Sikh shrines (successful Gurdwara Act 1925) and regarding itself as the voice of Sikhism, especially in political matters. Britain and other countries in which Sikhs have settled have an elected body, the Shiromani Akali Dal
akhand path	a continuous reading of the Guru Granth Sahib, taking forty-eight hours. Associated with occasions of great sorrow or joy and a means of observing Sikh festivals (gurpurbs)
amrit	nectar of immortality. Name given to sugar crystals (patasha) and water solution used at the initiation (pahul) ceremony
ananda	bliss, a quality or attribute of God and therefore of one who has realized moksha
Ardas	an important Sikh prayer used at the conclusion of a service
Baisakhi	first month of the year, according to some Indian calendars. Spring harvest. One of the great Sikh festivals marked by an animal fair at Amritsar

101

balihari	sacrifice, supreme devotion
bani	speech, confined to the compositions of the Gurus and the other bhagats included in the Guru Granth Sahib
bedi	the jati or clan of Guru Nanak, belonging to the kshatrya varna
bhagat	a devotee or exponent of bhakti. Used as a general term for the Hindu and Muslim sants whose compositions are included in the Guru Granth Sahib
bhai	brother, normally restricted to describing men of outstanding piety in the Sikh faith, e.g. Bhai Buddha, Bhai Gurdas
bija mantra	seed mantra, basic thought form
brahmin	the priestly class of Hindu society
chakra	wheel or circle, the six centres in the spinal column which are opened by hatha yoga in the process of realizing enlightenment
charn pahul	foot initiation. The foot of the guru is placed in water which is then given to the initiate to drink and/or is sprinkled on his face, eyes and hair. The Sikh method of initiation until it was replaced by khande de pahul, also known as khande ka amrit
charn puja	foot worship, touching or kissing the feet; performed by anyone to his social or family superior (e.g. son to father) or as a sign of respect (e.g. to an elderly person) but especially by a disciple to his guru. The idea lies behind the custom of many Sikhs to touch the step of the gurdwara upon entering it
chattri	umbrella, canopy of Guru Granth Sahib, symbol of honour
chela	the disciple of a guru, used as a synonym for sishya
dakshina	a voluntary fee given to a guru or to a priest for performing some rite or giving instruction
darshan	view, vision; sight of a holy person or important person (e.g. King-Emperor George V) believed to bestow spiritual power or virtue
das	slave, often suffix to a name of a devotee, e.g. Tulsi Das, Ram Das
dasam duar	tenth door, the other nine being the natural openings of the body. The tenth is a mystical one to perfect bliss
Dasam Granth	collection of writings attributed to the tenth Guru and made by Bhai Mani Singh twenty or thirty years after the Guru's death
dharmsala	commonly a hostel or inn. Among namdhari Sikhs a place of worship which has not been visited by a Guru

diksha	initiation of a disciple by a guru, often including the giving of a mantra
Diwali	a major Hindu festival falling at the beginning of the light part of the month Kartick (October–November). A time of Sikh assembly
diwan	court, name given to a Sikh act of worship
flag: nishan sahib	a saffron or blue flag bearing the Sikh symbols of the chakra and khanda should be flown from a high point on every gurdwara to indicate a rallying point for Sikhs and a place of shelter for travellers
gadi (gaddi)	seat or throne of a guru
Gayatri	the most famous example of a mantra, called 'the mother of the Vedas' and found in the Rig Veda 3.62.10
giani (gyani)	a person well-read in the Sikh scriptures, a teacher
Gorakh	literally, supporter of the earth a thirteenth-century yogi around whom many legends have accrued, reputed to be one of the nine perfect ones (siddhas) who have attained immortality
gosht	a discourse
Govind	literally, giver of enlightenment
granth	collection
granthi	one who looks after the Guru Granth Sahib (and should therefore be able to read it) and who may also be custodian of the gurdwara
gurdwara	literally, the door of the guru, consequently a building in which the scriptures are housed. May refer to a room in a private house or to a place of public worship
gurmukh	literally, the guru's word. One who follows the guru
Gurmukhi	the script in which the Guru Granth Sahib is written
gurpurb	anniversary of the birth or death of a guru, usually observed by an akhand path
guru	literally, gu means 'darkness', ru means 'light'; so one who delivers a person from ignorance by giving him the message which liberates and the technique to realize it
gurukripa	the grace of the guru
gurupades	the teaching of the guru
hatha-yoga	yoga of force. Regarded frequently in the West as physical exercises of a complex nature. In Hinduism these are a means to the progressive release of stores of psychic energy
haumai	self, self-centredness, a word which sums up the nature of unregenerate man
haveli	a large house, mansion
hukam	order, command, used in Qur'an 18[26]

janam sakhi	a tradition biography, literally birth evidences or life evidences
jap	repetition–of the name of God or of a mantra
jat	a Punjabi Sikh peasant class
jatha	Sikh fighting group in the eighteenth century; group of musicians; group of Sikhs organized to perform an akhand path
jathedar	leader of a jatha; now granthi of one of the four takhts
julaha	weaver jati to which Kabir belonged, officially regarded as Muslim
kach, kacha	short trousers worn instead of the dhoti, one of the five Ks
Kaliyug, Kalyug	the fourth and last cosmic age, literally related to the losing throw at dice. Kali means 'strife', 'battle'. Sometimes writers describe the Kalyug as the age of iron following the Greek tradition. The age is supposed to last for 432,000 years and is characterized by the deficiency of dharma. Instead of karma-marga and jnana-marga, bhakti-marga will be that most followed
kangha	comb; one of the five Ks
kara	the steel band worn on the right wrist; one of the five Ks
karah parshad	parshad (the gift of God to his devotees) prepared in an iron bowl (karah). Made of flour, sugar and ghee in equal proportions. Shared at the end of Sikh gatherings to symbolize casteless equality and brotherhood
karahi	iron bowl
kesh	uncut hair; one of the five Ks
keshadari	literally, one who wears the hair long or uncut. An initiated Sikh
Khalsa	the Pure Ones. The brotherhood of initiated Sikhs
Khalsa Diwan	the name give to the Singh Sabha of Amritsar founded in 1883
khanda	the double-edged sword; one of the emblems of Sikhism
khande ka amrit	Sikh form of initiation introduced by Guru Gobind Singh in 1699
khuda	one of the names used by Muslims for God–the Holy, al-Quddus
kirpan	sword; one of the five Ks
kirtan	singing of songs in praise of God, normally to the accompaniment of music
kshatriya	traditionally the warrior class of Hindu society
kundalini	the sakti or spirit of power which, when awakened by yoga, leads to illumination and control of hidden forces

104

langar	free kitchen instituted by Guru Nanak, perhaps influenced by Sufism
mahant	head of a religious institution or monastery, used of those who controlled gurdwaras
maharaja, maharajah	title given to an Indian ruler
mala	rosary of woollen cord, sometimes called a seli
man (mun)	mind
manji	small string bed (charpoy), used of twenty-two areas of jurisdiction established by Guru Amar Das
manmukh	one who follows the guidance of his own mind rather than that of the guru
mantra	word or verse often believed to confer power and insight upon the one who possesses it; given by a guru when a chela is initiated
massand	authorized leaders of local assemblies of Sikhs
maya	the natural world, created by God and therefore real, but capable of distracting man from God-centredness. The five vices are part of maya
misl	a file in which a record is kept; Sikh regiment
mool	basic
nam	name
nath	literally, 'music'. A yoga sect following Shaivite and Tantric Buddhist teachings. The traditional founder of the school was Siva
nihang	soldier-devotees, protectors of the gurdwaras
nirguna	unconditioned, without qualities
nitnam	daily 'prayer book' containing important sabads
pagri	turban
Panth	literally path, road. The total Sikh community
param	supreme
patasha	sugar crystals used in preparing amrit
pauri	stanza (literally, 'staircase') of a hymn ascending to a climax of praise
Prahlada	pious son of King Hiranya-Kasipu whose attempt to kill his son prompted Vishnu's fourth descent in the Sat Yug (First Age) as the Man-Lion
pranayam	yogic technique of breath control
prasad	gift received by devotee at worship
prasadi	grace
purana	eighteen books containing the mythology of Hinduism and regarded as important guides to behaviour
pyare	beloved
rag	musical form
Ram Chandra	Rama the charming, seventh avatar of Vishnu
Rama	seventh avatar of Vishnu, used as a name for God in the Guru Granth Sahib

rasayana	alchemy; transmuting of a base metal into gold through use of a chemical derived from mercury (rasa). It parallels the aim of nath-yogi through hatha-yogi
rishi	sage, usually a hermit
sach	true
sadhana	spiritual discipline ordered by a guru
saguna	with form or qualities, used of God
sahaj	ultimate state of mystical union
sampradaya	school, sect, tradition
sangat	gathering, congregation of Sikhs
sant	popularly a synonym for sadhu. In the context of Sikhism a member of the north Indian tradition to which Kabir and Nanak belonged
sanyasin	someone initiated into an ascetic order
Sat Guru	God
satsang, sat sangat	true fellowship, true community, i.e. the Sikh
shabad	word
shakti	energy of God expressed in his feminine counterpart
shaktipat	transfer of divine energy from guru to disciple
shastras	Hindu codes of conduct
Shromani Gurdwara Parbhandak Committee	committee responsible for looking after historic gurdwaras in the Punjab (Punjab, Haryana, Himalchalpradesh). Set up as a result of Gurdwara Act 1926
shudra	the lowest of the four orders of Hindu society
siddha	one of eighty-four perfected ones who gained immortality through yoga. Often confused with nath in Sikh writings
sishya	disciple
slok	complete stanza
smarta	follower of smrti, the Sanskrit tradition (as opposed to vernacular teachings)
smrti	that which has been remembered
sodhi	kshatriya sub-caste to which the last seven gurus belonged
srti	that which has been heard; revealed scripture
takht	throne; one of the four seats of Sikh religious authority
tantra	texts enunciating the forms of sakti worship
tenth door	(dasam dvar), the mystical opening to ultimate beatitude
tirath	a place of pilgrimage
trimurti	'triple form', the three aspects of divinity, creative, preserving and destructive; often personified in Brahma, Vishnu and Siva
udasi	(1) order of ascetics claiming Shri Chand, son of Guru Nanak, as their founder; (2) journey, preaching tour

vaisya	the third order of the twice-born classes. Its main responsibility being the provision of sacrificial offerings
Var	ode, eulogy
varnashram dharma	code of conduct laid down in the shashtras
Wahe-Guru	'Wonderful Lord'. Popular Sikh name for God. According to one tradition, formed from the initial letters V (Vishnu), A (Allah), H (Hari).

Bibliography

Allchin, F. R., *Kavitavali*. London 1964

Archer, J. C., *The Sikhs*. Princeton 1946

Avtar Singh, *Ethics of the Sikhs*. Patiala 1970

Basham, A. L., *The Wonder That Was India*. London 1970

Bhandarkar, R. G., *Vaisnavism, Saivism and Minor Religious Systems* (Collected Works, vol. 4). Poona 1929

Brent, P., *Godmen of India*, (Penguin edn). London 1972

Carpenter, J. G., *Theism in Medieval India*. London 1921

– *Cultural Heritage of India*, vols. 3 and 4 (2nd edn). Calcutta 1956

Cole, W. O., and Sambhi P. S., *The Sikhs*. London 1978

Cunningham, J. D., *A History of the Sikhs (Indian edn)*. Delhi 1960

Daniélou, A., *Hindu Polytheism*. New York 1964

Darsam Singh, *Indian Bhakti Tradition and the Sikh Gurus*. Chandigarh 1968

Dasgupta, S., *A History of Indian Philosopy*. Cambridge 1922–5

– *An Introduction to Tantric Buddhism*. Calcutta 1958

De Bary, W. T. (ed.), *Sources of Indian Tradition*. Columbia 1958

Farquhar, J. N., *Primer of Hinduism*. London 1912

Ghurye, S. S., *Indian Sadhus*, (2nd edn). Bombay 1967

Gopal Singh, *Guru Gobind Singh*. New Delhi 1966

Grewal, J. S., *Guru Nanak in History*. Chandigarh 1969

Grewal, J. S. and Bal, S. S., *Guru Gobind Singh*. Chandigarh 1967

– *Guru Nanak*. New Delhi 1969

– *Guru Nanak: Life, Times and Teachings*. New Delhi 1969

– *Guru Nanak: A Homage*. New Delhi 1973

Grierson, G. and Barnett, L. D., *Lalla Vakyani*. London 1920

Harbans Singh (ed.), *Perspectives on Guru Nanak*. Patiala 1975

Harnam Singh, *The Japji*. New Delhi 1957

Hastings, J., *Encyclopaedia of Religion and Ethics*. London 1925

Hinnells, J. H. and Sharpe, E. G., *Hinduism*. London 1972

Jogendra Singh, *Sikh Ceremonies*. Bombay 1941

Juergensmeyer, M. and Barrier, N. G., *Sikh Studies*. Berkeley 1979

Keay, F. G., *Kabir and His Followers*. Calcutta 1931

108

Khushwant Singh, *History of the Sikhs,* 2 vols. Oxford 1966. Indian edn, New Delhi 1977

Kohli, S. S., *Critical Study of the Adi Granth.* New Delhi 1966

– *Outlines of Sikh Thought.* New Delhi 1966

Ling, T. O., *History of Religion East and West.* London 1968

Loehlin, C. H., *The Christian Approach to the Sikh.* London 1966

– *The Granth of Guru Gobind Singh and the Khalsa Brotherhood.* Lucknow 1971

Macauliffe, M. A., *The Sikh Religion.* Oxford 1909. Reprinted 1963

McLeod, W. H., *Guru Nanak and the Sikh Religion.* Oxford 1968

– *Evolution of the Sikh Community.* Oxford 1976

– *The Early Sikh Tradition.* Oxford 1980

McMullen C. O. (ed.), *The Nature of Guruship.* New Delhi 1976

Mansukhani, G. S., *Guru Nanak.* New Delhi 1974

– *Quintessence of Sikhism* (2nd edn). Amritsar 1965

Mohan Singh, *A History of Punjabi Literature.* Amritsar 1956.

– *Kabir and the Bhagti Movement,* vol. 1, *Kabir – His Biography.* Lahore 1934

Narang, G. C., *Transformation of Sikhism* (5th edn). New Delhi 1960

Noss, J. D., *Man's Religions.* New York 1963

Parkash Singh, *Guru Nanak and His Japji.* Amritsar 1969

Parrinder, E. G., *Avatar and Incarnation.* London 1970

– *Worship and the World's Religions.* London 1974

Pritam Singh Gill, *Trinity of Sikhism.* Jullundur 1973

Pocock, J., *Mind, Body and Wealth.* Oxford 1974

– *Rehat Maryada.* English trans. 1970

Renou, L., *Religions of Ancient India.* London 1953

Rose, H. A., *Glossary of Tribes and Castes of the Punjab and North West Frontier,* 3 vols., reprinted. Chandigarh 1970

Sen K. M., *Hinduism.* London 1961

Sher Singh, *Philosophy of Sikhism.* Lahore 1944

– *Sikhism.* Patiala 1969

– *The Sikh Religion: A Symposium,* reprinted Calcutta 1958

Smart, N., *Religious Experience of Mankind.* New York 1969

Taran Singh, *Guru Nanak: Indian Religious Thought.* Patiala 1970

Teja Singh, *Growth of Responsibility in Sikhism.* Bombay 1948

– *Sikhism, Its Ideals and Institutions.* Lahore 1938

Thomas, Terry, *The Voice of the Guru.* Open University 1978

Trilochan Singh, *Guru Nanak.* New Delhi 1938

Vaudeville, C., *Kabir.* Oxford 1974

Verme, K., *Guru Nanak and the Gospel of the Divine Logos.* Allahabad 1969

Walker, B., *Hindu World.* London 1968

Westcott, G. H., *Kabir and the Kabir Panth*. Cawnpore 1907
Wilson, H. H., *Religious Sects of the Hindus*. (2nd edn). Calcutta 1958
Zaehner, R. C., *Hinduism*. Oxford 1962
– *Hindu Scriptures*. London 1966

Journals and Periodicals
Papers on Guru Nanak, Punjab History Conference. Patiala 1970
Parkh, *Punjabi Language and Literature Research Bulletin*, Chandigarh
  University
Punjab Past and Present, vol. 3. Patiala 1969
The Sikh Review
The Spokesman Weekly
The Spokesman Weekly, Anniversary Numbers

The Sikh Scriptures
Khushwant Singh, *The Hymns of Guru Nanak*. London 1969
Manmohan Singh, *Sri Guru Granth Sahib*, 8 vols. Amritsar 1962–9
Trumpp, E., *The Adi Granth* (reprinted). New Delhi 1970
UNESCO, *The Sacred Writings of the Sikhs*. London 1966

Index

Adi Granth 8, 13, 20, 26, 37, 77;
 compilation of 19, 55–6, Dam
 Dama recension 57, installed as
 Guru 58; doctrinal authority 77
 at assemblies of the Sarbat
 Khalsa 81
Aiteraya Upanishad 2
Akalis (eighteenth century) 80
Akbar, emperor 25, 26, 28, 75
akhand path 61
Allchin, Raymond 10
Amar Das, Guru 20, 24, 25, 50,
 65, 71
amrit 69, 70
Amritsar 58, 64, 82
Anand 69
Anand Marriage Act 83
Anandpur 67
anavi initiation 6
Angad, Guru 20, 23, 24, 36, 37,
 45, 69, 73; installed by Guru
 Nanak 36, 73
Angiras 3
Arjan, Guru 19, 20, 21, 24, 25, 26,
 27, 28, 29, 37, 44, 53, 55, 58, 65,
 75, 87, 88; attitude to birth of
 his son 27
Arjuna, king 3
Ardas, reminiscent of Arti
 ceremony 62
Arti (Arati) 23
Arya Samaj 82, 83
Atharva Veda 23
asana 6
avatar 31, 36, 38, 39, 44, 100; Sikh
 attitude to 36, 98, 99

Babur, emperor 28
Bahadur Shah, emperor 76
Baisakhi 34, 67, 68
Bal, S.S. 68, 71
Banda Singh (Banda Bahadur)
 76–7
Banerjee, I. 22, 69
bani *see* gurbani
bards, Sikh 30, 44, 55; *see also* Bal;
 Satta and Balwand
Bedi family 33
bedi-khatri 4, 33
Bein, river 15
bhagat bani 21
Bhagavad Gita 3, 31, 34
Bhai Banno 56–7
Bhai Buddha 26
Bhai Gurdas 21, 22, 23, 26, 36, 37,
 51
Bhai Mani Singh 56
bhajans 49
bhakti 49, 58
bhangi caste 11
Bidhi Chand 9
Brahma 28, 31, 40, 97
Brahma, as Adi Guru 3
Brahman 3, 43, 44, 99
Brahmin 3, 13–14, 71; Buddhist
 interpretation 4
Brihadaranyuka Upanishad 2
Buddha 4
Buddhism 4, 40

caste 3, 13, 64, 71; Sikh rejection
 of 28, 64–5
Chamkaur 76
Chandu 75–6

111